EMPLOYMENT GROUPS:

THE COUNSELLING CONNECTION

co-authored by

William A. Borgen

Diane E. Pollard

Norman E. Amundson

Marvin J. Westwood

Department of Counselling Psychology
University of British Columbia

LUGUS

Canadian Cataloguing in Publication Data

Main entry under title:

Employment groups : the counselling connection

Includes bibliographical references
ISBN 0-921633-64-5

1. Unemployed – Counseling of. 2. Small groups.
3. Group relations training. I. Borgan, William A.

HD5708.E5 1989   331.13'7   C89-095295-7

Published by Lugus Productions Ltd.
in co-operation with Employment and Immigration Canada, and
the Canadian Government Publishing Centre,
Supply and Services Canada

Catalogue Number MP43 – 228/1988E

SPECIAL THANKS

We are pleased to acknowledge the enormous assistance of Joan Hearn. Her specialist knowledge of both counselling and the English language has contributed tremendously to this book.

We are grateful to CEIC for assigning her as our project director for the development of this book because of her charming blend of critical thinking and constructive criticism.

ACKNOWLEDGMENTS

The preparation of this book has involved the assistance and support of a number of people. The special role of Joan Hearn has already been mentioned. In addition, André Paquin has helped guide the project while Lynne Bezanson and Valerie Ward have offered constructive and specific feedback.

Our thanks are also extended to the typists—Devona Shannon, Wendy Johnston, Ilona St. Anne, and Bay Gumboc—who worked long hours to meet very short deadlines.

Finally thanks to our families who were understanding and supportive throughout.

PREFACE

"You know more than you think you do." (*B. Spock*)

These famous and comforting words apply in an important way to you as you begin your study of group counselling because, of course, everyone has been a member of a group.

As we describe the ways groups grow and develop, and the ways people behave in them, you will find many points of reference to your own life experience. We have all been in groups and felt anxious or enthusiastic, smart or dumb, left out or "in like Flynn." You will certainly recognize many of the roles described: the class cut-up (Tension Reliever), the person who was always on your side (Encourager), the kid who had the most fascinating excuses for not having done the homework (Special Interest Pleader), the person who sat at the back of the class and made cynical remarks or perpetrated practical jokes to gain attention (the Grandstander), some of them familiar since our earliest experiences with groups.

You have also observed innumerable group leaders: teachers, scout or guide leaders, chair people, supervisors, team captains and so on. From your experience with all these people you have a good idea of what a group leader does—you are far from embarking on a journey into unknown territory.

As you contemplate your future as a group leader, an important, comforting principle to bear in mind is that you don't have to do it alone. You may be worried that you are going to be responsible for everything that happens. that the group is, as it were, a clean slate which your skills alone wlll transform either into a great work of art or perhaps something less exciting. But that is not the case. As you observe successive groups come to life you will notice that each one is different, but always, members have strengths as well as weaknesses and what they may contribute will add enormously to what the group will become and what it will accomplish. Each group as the sum (or, if you like, more than the sum) of its parts has a character and a strength of its own. To what you, as the leader, may do: encourage, empathize, support or challenge, the group can bring increased power. It can do this sometimes because there is simply a greater array of resources present, but the larger reason is that, first and last, we are all social beings and groups are very important to us.

Developing the leadership skills for group employment counselling is a challenge, but it is one which is well worth the effort. It is important to remember when embarking on this journey that much of your learning in Modules I and II will be directly transferable to your work in groups. It will be written about in slightly different terms but the parallels will be clear. There will be a few new communication skills to add to those you have learned and you will be able to adapt some you already know to the groups' situation. That being so, it is important still to keep in mind the special nature of group counselling which does not simply repeat the procedures of individual counselling with a collection of individuals. The interaction of members and the resources they bring to one another provide many new opportunities.

How to work with these opportunities as a group leader is what the rest of this book is all about.

CONTENTS

Chapter 1

Introduction

Each of us is a member of many groups: of a family, of a work group and of a friendship group, to name only three examples. Much of what we learn about ourselves comes from group interaction. Much of what we believe about ourselves, feel about ourselves, is formed from the feedback received from members of groups to which we have belonged.

According to the psychologist, Alfred Adler, humans are social beings who develop a sense of meaning within the context of the group. Social psychologists Johnson & Johnson (1982, p. 2) state explicitly that, "as the effectiveness of our groups goes, our quality of life goes...The effectiveness of our groups depends, both on our knowledge of group processes and our ability to behave effectively within groups."

A group is constantly in motion, dynamic and multidimensional. There is also a paradox: people like to be in groups—if Adler is correct, they are only fully human in a group—and yet within the group, they need to be recognized as unique individuals and possessed of a special value, as, in fact, they are.

We hope that, in reading this book and participating in the training to follow, you will find Group Employment Counselling to be a challenging and exciting approach to assisting unemployed people. The challenge of leading groups requires you to add group counselling knowledge to the assessment and individual counselling techniques you already possess (Modules I and II). The excitement is that group work will open up a way to offer clients an efficient and secure environment in which to make career and employment decisions, to master the skills required to find and keep a job and even to find a new world of work.

This self study manual has two major purposes:

1. **to provide a systematic understanding of group processes and development, and**

2. **to provide an understanding of the importance of leadership and how the leader must function within the group context.**

A WORKING DEFINITION OF A GROUP

Authors tend to describe groups within the various contexts in which group counselling strategies are used. The definition most appropriate in a group employment counselling setting is that suggested by Johnson & Johnson (1982):

> A group may be defined as two or more individuals who (a) interact with each other, (b) are interdependent, (c) define themselves and are defined by others as belonging to the group, (d) share norms concerning matters of common interest and participate in a system of interlocking roles, (e) influence each other, (f) find the group rewarding, and (g) pursue common goals. (p.7)

A clear example, possibly the first which came to mind when you read this definition, is some kind of sports team— especially because of the reference to pursuing common goals. The idea is still fairly clear if you think of the group of individuals with whom you work even if, on your cynical days, you feel more as if you are playing for Charlie Brown than for the captain of the Montreal Expos.

The types of groups we will be emphasizing in this text are learning groups with the same kind of psycho-educative emphasis found in Modules I and II. This means a focus on the individual psychological make-up of each client plus what that client and collectively, these clients, need to learn or re-learn. Unemployed people can be effectively helped in a structured learning group where the primary focus is on exploration, learning job-search skills and developing the sense of self confidence necessary to carry out and maintain a prolonged and effective job search. As you know, there are other kinds of groups: personal development groups, therapy groups and so on. Some of the good things which happen in those groups may happen incidentally in a learning group: insights which have a therapeutic result or personal development, and if so, that will be wonderful—but definitely a bonus. Neither the mandate of the CEIC or your training justify any goals but learning.

You will therefore, notice in the description to come of these groups that there are two emphases: acquisition of relevant skills and information, which is the "educative" element, and the development and/or maintenance of a constructive attitude (so often impeded by emotions which must be recognized: anxiety, fear and depression). The development of this attitude, the "psycho" part of "psycho-educative," can greatly facilitate the task at hand.

Knowledge of groups is essential, but it is not enough to produce a proficient leader. As leader of an employment group, you not only need a functional understanding of group dynamics and structure, but you must also have an ability to work within the group context. In other words, you need the skills that help groups function effectively.

All of this can sound like a pretty tall order and may make you question whether or not you can be an effective group leader. You may have had some of the same doubts before you entered Modules I and II.

In order to help you take a clear look at some of the issues that often bother people about leading groups, we have put together a list of the questions most frequently raised, plus the answers. Our purpose is to help de-bunk some myths about groups and to provide you with a picture of what you might realistically expect.

1. Are groups difficult to manage: can you have control taken away by certain members who may be in the group?

The number one fear, client "take-over," *can* happen to leaders who do not have the necessary training and background.

To be honest, client take-over used to happen a lot back in the days when the general view was that anyone could run a group and that no training was necessary. Experience has changed this view. Experience has also provided a body of knowledge and techniques which minimize the grounds for this fear. Knowledge about group member selection and structuring of the group sessions added to basic practice in leading a group, can create a situation where group members will respond well to direction. Within a brief period of time, group members can assume responsibility for their own behaviour and individual goal attainment in the group. At this point, the need for counsellor "control" has obviously disappeared.

In fact, the idea of "control" is a contentious one in group counselling. No one wants a group, "out of control," a frightening idea which is really behind the whole question of the "take-over." On the other hand, no one wants a group "under control" (unless, of course, you are a sergeant in the armed forces) with its suggestion of rigidity and a lack of personal freedom or creativity.

The answer lies in a balance between sensitive leadership, well thought-out design and structured learning activities.

Limits and rules for monitoring and guiding individual member behaviour can also be established in order that the leader is free to observe the group, direct or intervene when appropriate.

2. Is counselling people in groups much more difficult than counselling them in a one-to-one situation?

Only if you lock yourself into the sergeant-major role we mentioned above.

Leading a group is enjoyable and exciting. Once a group is established and running, you may find your role in the group less stressful than it is in one-to-one counselling interviews. You can gain a deep sense of satisfaction and accomplishment when you see that you have been successful in teaching group members how to assist one another in meeting their goals of improved self-confidence (for example).

3. Do groups tend to be process in nature and concentrate on member feelings instead of member goals?

You can have the kind of group you need.

Research evidence suggests that clients perceive effective employment counselling groups as providing key information related to job search and providing an appropriate level of personal support. The accumulated resource base of the group allows a richer fund of task and support-focused activities for members than would be possible in an individual counselling setting.

Group processes can never be ignored, but in employment counselling, it serves to support the acquisition of knowledge and skills for employment-related purposes and can never be an end in itself - as it often is in a therapeutic (psychiatric) setting.

4. Can group counselling be more effective in helping clients achieve their goals than one-to-one counselling?

We are enthusiastic about groups, but no single means of helping people is a panacea and we obviously don't make any such a claim for the group approach. Obviously, choice of counselling approach depends on client need. The fact is that many clients do much, much better within the social context of the group which can provide support, understanding and motivation to help them achieve their own goals. More specifically, the group setting allows members to observe how their experience of unemployment may be similar to or different from that of other people. In addition, the group provides a realistic setting for the practice of new skills within a supportive environment.

Unquestionably, there are people who, in your judgment, will not do well in a group. A client with a language difficulty would be an obvious example. Some clients, you might believe, will be very destructive in a group setting; in that case, no one gains anything.

5. Are groups used primarily for clients who need group therapy rather than counselling?

Groups can be established with a variety of different objectives and for a range of different populations.

Contrary to what all the hoopla that has surrounded this subject in the past may have led you to believe, education and training-based groups are the norm, rather than the exception in human services in North America. Group counselling, unlike group therapy, uses a problem solving, psycho-educative or education-based foundation.

Groups in an employment counselling setting are for people who are functioning "normally" and who are obliged to cope with the crisis of unemployment, rather than for individuals who require special services of a psychotherapeutic nature.

6. Properly set up and run, are groups more time efficient and economical as a delivery system than multiple counselling on a one-to-one interview basis?

Yes.

Research findings indicate that when groups have been well designed and conducted, more people with a common goal are assisted in a shorter time span than may be possible by working with the same number of people on an individual basis.

Chapter 2

Running Groups for Unemployed Clients: Background Information

OVERVIEW

Chapter I provided a general description of groups along with a general discussion of the ways in which groups constitute an effective counselling approach. The purpose of this chapter is to provide you with some of the research evidence that points to the effectiveness of groups in assisting unemployed people, the ways in which groups are particularly helpful in meeting the needs of people who are out of work.

OBJECTIVES

Upon successful completion of this chapter it is expected that you will be competent to:

1. **list the factors that may influence people's reactions to unemployment,**

2. **describe ways in which unemployment affects people's abilities to meet their needs, and**

3. **explain the factors which contribute to the success of employment counselling groups.**

FACTORS THAT INFLUENCE THE EXPERIENCE OF UNEMPLOYMENT

Unemployment affects the lives of people in many different ways. Clearly, unemployment changes people's financial status, but it may also influence friendship patterns, and may significantly alter career paths. These changes, in turn, both cause and reflect a dramatic shift in the capacity people have to meet their needs and cope on a day-to-day basis. The end result of this is that people often fall into an emotional roller coaster which detracts from their job search, both how they carry it out and whether they have the energy to carry it out at all. It affects whether they can sustain a positive self-concept, feel good about themselves or whether they indulge in miserable bouts of self-loathing. All of this material, you will recall, was described in detail in Module II.

In more recent studies, individuals caught in the emotional turmoil which characterizes unemployment, have been able to identify factors which help them to cope and factors which destroy this ability. (Amundson & Borgen, 1987).

Obviously, these factors constitute significant information for employment counsellors, both those designing counselling interventions and those working with groups. Several of these factors are rank ordered below:

Positive Factors	*Negative Factors*	*
1. Support from family,	1. Job rejections,	*
2. Support from friends,	2. Financial pressure,	*
3. Positive thinking,	3. Contact with agencies,	*
4. Career changes; plans for retraining,	4. Future unknown or negative,	*
5. Part-time or temporary work,	5. Job search activities,	*
6. Job search/support groups; vocational counselling,	6. Thinking negatively,	*
7. Initial job search; making job contacts,	7. Spouse or family problems.	*
8. Physical activity.		*

The bases which underlie positive and negative factors can be * understood by considering the fundamental human needs which * have been identified by Alvin Toffler (1980), namely, the need * for community: a sense of belonging, being part of a larger * whole (family, friends, and, of course, work); meaning: making a * contribution, being valued (and, sometimes, in our day, having * money) and structure: a guaranteed schedule for the day, * predictability, consistency in day-to-day living and the sense of * safety which goes with these. Many of the factors identified as * being positive help people to meet their needs for community * (support from family and friends, a sense of being valued and * respected in a group context), meaning (thinking positively, * part-time or temporary work) and structure (making job * contacts, part-time or temporary work, physical activity). Of * particular significance in the list of positive factors is the * mention of job search/support groups. Nearly everyone who was * a member of a job search support group found the experience to * be a useful one. *

In looking at the list of negative factors it becomes evident * that many of these factors detract significantly from the ability of * people to meet their needs for community (spouse/family * problems) and meaning (job rejection, future unknown or * negative, thinking negatively, financial pressures). And although * a lack of structure is not specifically identified, the statements of * some individuals to the effect that, for example, they insulate * themselves from reality by sitting in front of the television all day, * indicate how negative a lack of structure can be. Nothing to do * and all day to do it in. These factors constitute a sort of negative, * mirror-image of the positive factors. *

The clear identification of these positive and negative factors, by victims of unemployment, suggests that it is essential to consider these basic human needs when developing counselling interventions. There is also more than a suggestion that group employment counselling can provide an excellent vehicle by which to offer service to unemployed people.

EVIDENCE IN SUPPORT OF GROUP EMPLOYMENT COUNSELLING

There is ample evidence to show that group counselling can be effective with a variety of client populations facing a huge diversity of problem issues. Help with problems around unemployment and/or job search issues is a prominent and very successful example. A summary of this evidence suggests that groups offer an effective and efficient way to assist people in meeting needs for community, meaning and structure—whatever the particular subject or nature of their problems.

Research that we conducted (Amundson & Borgen, 1986) outlines specifically the particular benefits of participating in a job search group. One subject summed up his experience in a way that says it all:

Male, single, 23 years, labourer

"It was really worthwhile being in the group because it gave me something to do every day. You get up in the morning and you have somewhere to go. You felt like you were accomplishing something. You just weren't wasting your time. When you came down to the group, everybody was trying to help you and you were trying to help them." (Structure, meaning and community).

A more detailed analysis indicated that nineteen factors accounted for the success of the groups. Seventeen of these nineteen factors could be placed under the two general purposes described later in this chapter as being important in employment counselling groups: acquisition of relevant skills and infor- *
mation (Employment Orientation), and development/mainte- *
nance of a constructive attitude (Support/Self-Esteem). *

Employment Orientation

Factors here included all of those activities, plus straight information, which helped people meet their employment needs. An example of how helpful these activities were perceived to be is provided in the following quotation.

Male, married, 44 years, shipper receiver:

"Through the activities in the group I learned how to present myself better. I learned how to knock on the door, get past the receptionist and get to the personnel manager. I also learned how to develop a resumé, set up letters and do a follow-up."

Obviously the specific factors under this category may vary according to the purpose of the group (job search, career re-direction, etc.). In our study, where the groups surveyed were aimed at job search, the specific factors found to be helpful in carrying out needed tasks were:

- Job Search Strategies
- Videotape Feedback
- Telephone Techniques
- Interview Practice and Preparation
- Supplies and Service

- Goal Setting *
- Job leads *
- Information on the *
  labour market *
- Instruction (in writing) *
- Resumés and *
  correspondence *

Support/Self Esteem

A constellation of factors were cited as helping group members *
to feel connected to others and to gain the confidence and hope *
they needed to continue job search. Membership in the group *
helped people feel included and supported (obviously, community). Because members of the group were mutually interested in
what happened in each other's job search, people tended to acquire a sense of purpose and meaning derived, actually, from the
importance attached by other people. To say this is not to deny
that counsellors in the individual situation do project a very real
caring and concern, that they are totally on the client's side. Just
the same, the caring of peers, as it is encountered in the group,
often has that extra quality which is so characteristic of the group
experience—and so powerful.

Here are the factors persistently named as offering support and buildup of self-esteem:

- Belonging to the group   *
- Mutual support & encouragement   *
- Mutual communication of feelings of enthusiasm and   *
  success between members   *
- Comparison of situation with that of others   *
- Contribution to helping others (feeling valuable)   *
- Ventilating feelings   *
- Developing a positive outlook   *
- Supportive leader   *

The importance of these factors is well illustrated by one of the unemployed people in our study.

Female, separated, 29 years, bookkeeper

"It was nice being with other people. When you have a job you work with other people. When you're looking for a job it seems that you're all alone. There aren't a lot of encouraging things built into job search, especially if your interviews don't go well. You start to feel lousy after a while. In the group we worked together and shared the good and the bad experiences. We encouraged each other and we seemed to all have job prospects to pass on to each other. We became friends."

As you are already experienced in individual counselling, none of these findings will seem very exotic. You have worked with clients in matters of Employment Orientation. You have certainly been active in supporting and promoting client self-esteem, creating, through your own efforts and skill, the counselling conditions which are so productive.

All this is solid experience, well understood by you—a good basis from which to extrapolate to the group process.

One of the factors which was difficult to place in the Employ- *
ment Orientation or Support/Self Esteem categories was that of *
follow-up support and services. This factor seemed to apply to *
both categories and thus was not included in either list. The *
remaining factor seemed to stand on its own because the role of
structure is difficult to classify. A telling comment reflects its
importance.

Female, married, 54 years, dry cleaner

"Being in the group was like going to work. You knew that
you had to get up in the morning and be at class by a certain time. A number of hours of each day were committed
to being in that class. That alone, getting a routine into
your life really helps."

Observation indicates clearly that these factors do indeed
help people to meet their needs for community (belonging to
the group, mutual support, etc.), meaning(contribution to others, developing a positive outlook, goal setting), and structure
(routine).

Placing a value or rank ordering these factors is more
difficult. But what does seem evident is that while Employment
Orientation factors are essential, Support/Self Esteem factors
are equally essential. In fact, it probably would be more accurate
to describe the groups as "Job Search/Support Groups" in view
of the importance of the support dimension.

A very important additional research finding, which seems to
emphasize the role that support plays, is that people seemed to
benefit from their experience in the group regardless of whether
or not they found employment. Those who were still unemployed reported that they were able to maintain a more effective
job search and a positive self image as a result of their experiences in the groups. The simple fact that people had been in the *
group caused them to feel much better about themselves. *

In most cases, people indicated that a job search group would *
have been most helpful in the first three months of unemploy- *
ment. This finding certainly emphasizes the need to provide a *
job search/support group for the unemployed at the earliest *
opportunity. *

SUMMARY

The purpose of this chapter has been to provide some specific research evidence for the effectiveness of employment counselling groups. In addition, the information helped to refine the concept of a group by examining—in broad terms—what groups offer and why they are successful in the ways they are.

In Chapter I, we referred to the "Learning Group" which is a clear and close relative of the "psycho-educative" approach studied in Modules I and II. What is probably clear to you now, having read this chapter, is that people who feel supported, accepted, affirmed as "OK" people by their peers, learn better and (feel better) than people who feel rejected and unacceptable. Not so surprising. "Support" and "learning," then, are the two essential elements of the learning group. All the indications are that support is primary and learning follows on.

The purpose of the rest of the book is to help you understand the basic principles by which you may develop and lead such a group.

POINTS TO REMEMBER

- **Unemployed people experience a series of emotional reactions which involve (a) anger and sadness about job loss, and (b) determination, hope, fear, hopelessness and helplessness about job search. These feelings need to be understood and recognized as valid and very real.**

- **There are both positive and negative factors which can influence the way people experience unemployment. Positive factors tend to help people meet their needs for community, meaning and structure, while negative factors threaten their ability to meet these needs.**

- **Research has shown that groups can be an effective and efficient method of assisting unemployed clients. Groups having components that help people develop both job search skills and self-confidence are enjoyed by clients and seem highly effective.**

EXERCISES

1. From your experience and the information provided in the chapter, identify five important positive and negative factors that influence the way people experience unemployment.

2. Identify in the following quotations some of the needs that are unfulfilled as a result of these people losing their jobs:

a) *"I just don't see anyone anymore. When you don't have the money to go out there's really not much point in getting together. Everything costs money these days."*

Needs unmet:

b) *"It's not so much the money, it's more that I just don't have a place anymore. My kids have grown up and there's not much to do around the house. What good am I to anybody?"*

Needs unmet:

3. Identify, from the following quotations, the factors (listed on pages 8 and 9) which contribute to the success of a group.

a) *"I really learned a lot from using the videotape. It was good to see myself and get other ideas from others in the group."*

Factor(s):

b) *"I never realized how important it was to set up a good resumé. If that's not done well you might as well forget about your chances."*

Factor(s):

c) *"I really appreciated getting out of the house and working again with others. We had a job to do and it was important to be there every day and keep at it."*

Factor(s):

d) *"Sometimes I would really feel down, but the group kept me going. It is so important to have the right outlook. If you don't believe in yourself, no one else will."*

Factor(s):

5. What does recent research show about the results of being in a job search group for people who do not immediately find work?

Chapter 3

A Model for Group Employment Counselling

OVERVIEW

As the reader is aware from Modules I and II, the individual counsellor needs to operate within a theoretical counselling framework. As you study group employment counselling, you will operate from a system as well.

In this chapter we introduce a group counselling system model that is essential for understanding the functioning, structure and leadership of the group. This is "The Group Employment Counselling Model." Both the essential components of an effective group and the theory of group development are presented.

It is essential that you develop some familiarity with this model in order to understand what follows. We are sensitive, however, to the fact that the chapter contains a succession of ideas and explanations and they, in turn, are quite a lot to remember. Bear in mind that the material will be repeated in the rest of the text.

OBJECTIVES

After you have read this chapter, it is expected that you will be competent to:

1. outline the five major components of group employment counselling,

2. describe the relationship among the various components,

3. identify the six stages involved in organizing and running an effective employment counselling group,

4. describe the sequential nature of group development,

5. describe the basic group member needs for inclusion, control and trust; how these needs evolve through the stages of group development and how they influence group members' roles and behaviours.

THE MODEL

The model, presented here, is simply an analogy, a way of thinking about groups which our experience has shown to be useful for purposes of analysis and planning. Groups, as we said in Chapter 1, are never static but constantly in motion and multidimensional. A better illustration (although not a model) would be to think of the motion of atoms, constantly moving, bumping into and mutually changing each other at every encounter.

The model, like any drawing of an atom, is static, pinned down and therefore, easy to study. What it represents is not. "The Model," as you the group leader will live through and experience it, is fluid and dynamic but integrated. It is important for you to be aware of the interrelationships of Components with the Stage of group development. The Components are described first and the Stages will be explained later.

BASIC GROUP COMPONENTS

We have used the word "Component" to indicate a cluster or grouping of activities or skills, "elements" if you want to think in chemical terms, which combine to make a particular contribution, to constitute a particular function within the whole system which is group employment counselling.

Several components come into play and interact in all groups, regardless of their type or purpose. Five components which it is vital to understand in relation to the functioning of a successful group, are shown in the model.

Each component functions only in relation to the others. If a   *
change in one part of the system occurs, there will undoubtedly   *
be a reorganization of the entire system. This fact will be obvious   *
to you if you think of changing, say, the "Member" in *Member Needs and Roles* from disadvantaged youth, drop-outs with no work experience, to victims of a plant-closing.

The disadvantaged youth, being youth, will be much closer to adolescence and may still be having real trouble in relating to adults, which will include you. You will have to be careful, in your approach to leading, to avoid being cast in the authoritarian mold, which would be a wonderful excuse for more rebellious behavior, and, at the same time, to keep the group task-focused. Because adolescents, as a group, are noted for their tendency to be fairly self-absorbed, these members may need real help from you in learning to relate to and, in a caring way, for each other— a matter of group process. Activities can be varied and if they involve self-discovery, especially at the beginning, they will be followed with deep interest.

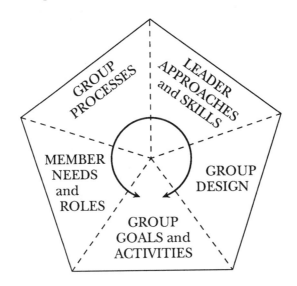

The victims of plant-closing you may find far from rebellious but heavily depressed. You may have to deal with a strong tendency to be dependent—to want you to have all the answers and to suppose that you do, and these expectations will certainly influence your approach. Activities will have to be very strictly goal-oriented but again you will have to be sure that members are not too depressed to participate. These people may, however, have a much clearer sense of all being in the same boat, communicate better, be more understanding and supportive toward each other. Therefore, your role as leader will not be perceived necessarily as authoritarian, but as helping.

What follows is a closer look at each component.

GROUP GOALS AND ACTIVITIES

All groups should have a set of goals that define their purpose, or raison d'être. Group members and you, the leader, bring to a group certain expectations. In order for the group to become effective, each individual's expectations must be integrated into a   *
set of goals which all members of the group can agree   *
upon—the group goals. These goals must then be broken down   *
into outcomes—standards (usually behavioural) which the group   *
will accept as indicating that the goals have been achieved.

Once the group goals have been defined, the group begins its work towards achievement of matching outcomes. The progression is shown below. First the Purpose of the group, "To get a job", is followed by the Goals "Learn how to do an effective interview" which will support the Purpose. So how about the Outcome? How will the group know the Goal has been accomplished? In this case the group decides upon "Demonstrate an effective job interview in front of the group," as the Outcome.

Purpose	Goals	Outcomes
To get a job	Learn how to do an effective interview	Demonstrate an effective job interview in front of the group

In order to reach its goals via its outcomes, a group needs to engage in a variety of structured learning activities. These activities become the key focus of the group. As we discussed in Chapter II, some activities will relate to the work that the group needs to perform in order to accomplish its goals while others will be about psychological support and self-esteem. Activities usually insert themselves into the Purpose-Goals-Outcomes chain like this:

Purpose	Goals	Activity	Outcome
To get a job	Learn how to do an effective interview	*Task focus:* Videotape practice of job interview *Maintenance focus:* Supportive feedback from other members	Demonstrate an effective job interview in front of the group

Excepting differences arising from the group context, the whole process of establishing goals and outcomes, selecting activities (a variation of strategies) is the same as it is in individual counselling. The structured learning activities that you set for the group reflect the group goals. These goals change over time as the group evolves and additional goals with a somewhat better "fit" for the group may emerge. For example: Some new Canadians have a cultural background which requires that a member of the family, usually a parent, accompanies a young person to a job interview. As participants learn more about the Canadian approach to job search, a new goal may emerge: how to tell family members that their presence will hinder, not help.

Group goals and the activities that they require are primary and integrating in the life of the group.

MEMBER NEEDS AND ROLES

Members of an employment counselling group arrive with two basic kinds of needs:

a) needs that make themselves felt because the individual is   *
unemployed, (described in the previous chapter), and,   *

b) needs that arise from being a group member.   *

While the first set of needs may vary from one individual to   *
another, the needs arising from being a group member are   *
consistent and predictable. Understanding both types of needs is   *
essential in leading a group. According to Schutz (1958), some   *
of the major needs which exist across the stages of group   *
development include the following: inclusion, control and trust.   *
We touch on them fairly superficially here, basically so that you   *
will recognize them when they turn up later.   *

It will be clear to you that these needs, as described here, could exist in the same way in an individual counselling relationship. They are a logical follow-on from some of the same general kinds of anxieties present in individual counselling: will the counsellor accept me? Is something bad going to happen? Can I trust this person? There are the same needs to feel safe and to be able to trust before being able to commit to change. And the same reluctance if the outlook seems threatening and insecure.

Inclusion refers to a group member's need to have a sense of be-   *
longing to the group. Failure to satisfy this need may give rise to   *
one or more of the following feelings: insecurity, feelings of rejection, anxiety and hurt. These feelings may be expressed through a variety of behavioural reactions which, taken together, may constitute a role. As an easy example, a group member who feels "included out" may react with silent behaviour and a persistent display of closed body posture: "the Withdrawer."

Control is defined as a group member's need to maintain a sense *
of being able to influence what happens to him/her and (some- *
times) others, in a group. The need to control or be controlled *
comes to the surface in issues related to who influences decisions
made by the group and the relative power of group members vis-
a-vis other members or the leader.

As the group evolves, concern with power or control is always
present, but the members change the ways in which they deal
with this concern, moving from initial dependency upon the
leader to rebellion/independency to interdependency among
themselves.

Members express their need for power/control in a variety of
ways resulting in the assumption of "roles" which reflect this
need. For example, some may demonstrate a high need to control others but strongly resist any control by others of themselves.
By contrast, some members may desire a lot of control or direction from others while not wanting to reciprocate by taking a
turn at controlling or checking themselves. In other words, some
group members prefer to lead while others prefer to follow. In
another example, the need for power (control) over others often
results from a feeling of inadequacy which may, in turn, be dis-
played behaviourally by putting others down. The role then may
be developed and played out in the group as the "group critic."

Trust refers to a group member's need to feel close to, and *
secure with other group members. The extent to which this need *
is met influences the degree to which members' relationships
become close in a group. Again, expression of this need can be
indirect and confusing for other people. Some members may
want to be in a close, trusting relationship with the other group
members but fail to express this need in a manner that will
encourage people to trust them. In a clearer example, a sense of
"closeness with others," may be expressed behaviourally in
empathic statements to other group members. The role then
could be played out as the person who tries to ensure that other
members all have a chance to speak, "the group gatekeeper."

The following illustration shows how member needs produce
first feelings and then behaviours which often turn into full-
blown roles.

Needs/Values	Behaviours		Roles
Belonging *INCLUSION*	General	Specific	
Feelings or thoughts are usually of a fear of rejection or of not being accepted	Behavior which may be to withdraw	Shows itself in silence, glancing or looking away	A typical role in this case is "the silent member."
Safety *CONTROL*			
Feeling is a desire for safety (nothing terrible will happen) and/or a worry about being inadequate	Behavior may be to put others down, keep them off balance so they will not do anything to threaten	Shows itself in verbal criticism, sarcasm, making fun, jeering at people, etc.	A typical role is "group critic."
Close Relationship *TRUST*			
Feeling is a desire for a "sense of closeness with others"	Behaviour of group member may be to join with another member by showing understanding	Shows itself in statement of empathy	A typical role is "gatekeeper."

GROUP PROCESSES

Group processes refer to those forces which influence how a *
group operates. The processes are the mechanisms which assists *
the group in moving ahead to complete its work. *
A simple analogy would be to a primitive engine. It is com- *
posed of parts such as gears, pistons, a drive shaft and so on, *
each of which, in action, accomplishes a function but one which *
must interact with the others to make the wheels go around so *
that the engine gets where it is going. *
Another analogy would be to think of the processes as mus- *
cles in the human body, which are many and varied. Each has a *
different function, but one or two alone are not much use, it is *
the interaction which gets people to their destinations. These *
destinations, these goals, are not inherent in the muscles, they *
come from the "mind" of the individual (or individuals), but the *
goals cannot be reached without the muscles. *
Key group processes include: communication, norm setting, *
decision making, confronting the problem, problem solving and *
conflict management. The designation "group processes" refers *
to all of the functioning "parts" which interacting together in a *
group may facilitate (or, alternatively, hinder) the group in *
achieving its goals. *

It is easy to see how interdependent all the components are if
you understand that a leader needs to be aware of and use a
variety of group processes to meet member needs for inclusion
and trust. In addition, you will need to help group members to
understand, and learn to assist in making group processes effective for all members.

In order to provide a clearer understanding of the central role
which group processes play in overall group functioning, let us
examine six processes. These processes will be described in more
detail as each stage of group development is presented in subsequent chapters of the book.

a) Communication

Communication skills, as you are well aware, clarify meaning and
improve mutual understanding. Counselling on a one-to-one

basis simply does not progress unless there is clear understanding. In fact, it can be argued that much of counselling consists of clearing away misunderstanding, bringing into focus previously fuzzy ideas and generally assisting thought. All the communication skills now at your disposal will also be used in group counselling. The difference is that they may often be used to improve understanding between members, to help them to build positive and productive relationships with each other as well as with the counsellor. Things get better because people work together— and the better people communicate the better they function.

If you teach, model and reinforce the use of specific communication skills, members will find that understanding each other, making decisions and building trust are easier than if no training is provided or if destructive communication is used. As an instance, by modelling paraphrasing and the use of empathy, (as opposed to making assumptions and evaluative statements, which is what members may do as the group begins) you will reduce the probability of interpersonal conflict developing. You will recall from your earlier training, the sorts of difficulties which unexamined assumptions engender. The kind of misleading, evaluative statements clients may make about themselves do not become more successful when applied to other people. What you model demonstrates the alternative.

b) Norms

All groups need a basic set of rules or guidelines to promote constructive interaction so that each member feels like an integral part of what is happening, has a sense of contributing to the group's work and feels safe. These rules are called norms. There are many kinds of norms and ways of describing them. Two key examples would be rules for guaranteeing confidentiality and rules for member-to-member feedback. Norms will be discussed in the course of describing each stage of group development in subsequent chapters.

c) Decision Making

Decision-making is a very important part of counselling and you will certainly recall, and probably often use, the decision model that is an important part of Module II. It is not inconceivable, in fact, that you may use the decision making balance sheet in your own life and you should certainly not abandon it as you approach group counselling.

A group certainly adds another dimension to decision-making, however, even though, as always, there are still several ways in which a decision may be made. The process of decision-making used by a group will be of particular importance to you, as you will need to help the members recognize the comparative effectiveness of different group decision making approaches within various contexts. A majority vote decision, for example, may be an appropriate approach for deciding on an issue of minor importance, such as "coffee break time". Consensus decision-making may be the best choice for an issue which is critically important to the members of the group; for instance, decisions on group goals or the procedures for giving feedback.

d) Confronting the Problem

This process is a mechanism which deals with feelings or behaviours of group members that are impeding group progress. It is most effective if there is immediate awareness (the leader must always be alert) and prompt action to address the feelings or behaviour which are reflecting the difficulty.

To refer back to the engine analogy, Confronting the Problem, has a filter functions: it prevents grit and pollutants from setting in and gumming up the works. Without this process being accomplished, small problems become big, your group is likely to develop funny noises, start spluttering and eventually grind to a halt.

It is crucial to get the issues out in the open. The practice of getting issues quickly "on the table" for discussion prevents some conflicts from arising, and all of them from escalating. Many different skills are used in getting the issue on the table: empathy, clarification, immediacy and mediation, for example.

Empathic confrontation—the only kind which should ever be used in counselling—is something with which you are familiar. Confronting the problem has many of the same qualities: highlighting the difference between what is supposed to be happening and what is happening, having people recognize this difference and that it gets in the way of the group's work. It is a necessity in goal-oriented counselling but it must be carefully handled as you will recall from your previous training.

e) Creative Conflict Resolution

This process becomes necessary when differences of opinion are "full blown." Two types of situations tend to create the need for creative conflict resolution. Both are peculiar to group (as opposed to individual) counselling. These are *controversies* and *conflicts of interest.*

Controversies involve differences of opinion regarding assumptions, beliefs, suggested plans of action, etc. The group leader uses the views expressed by members to generate a variety of possible solutions and actions. The results of turning a potentially negative situation into a means for further understanding of differing views and for suggesting a greater range of options are, often, more creative and constructive solutions.

Conflicts of interest arise when the needs of one group member directly interfere with the ability or capacity of another group member to meet his or her needs (e.g., when several group members are looking for the same type of job). In these situations you will be called upon to mediate conflicting needs.

To repeat: a group is dynamic, interactive and complex. A great deal of the dynamism, interaction and complexity is accounted for in terms of the group processes. Hence, an understanding of group processes is essential for effective leadership. Each of the group processes will be elaborated in more detail within the context of the Stages of group development.

LEADERSHIP: APPROACHES AND SKILLS

In employment counselling groups, you will be called upon to respond to members' needs by designing a group to meet these needs, by organizing and implementing these group activities, and by leading and monitoring group development. To meet *
these requirements you need first to acquire basic skills to *
complement those already learned in Modules I and II. *
Secondly, you must perform various skills to guide members *
through, and manage group interaction. *

The range of skills and approaches that you will need to know *
and understand as a group leader are so central and of such im- *
portance that they merit an entire chapter (the next one) to *
themselves. *

DESIGN

The difference between an effective and an ineffective group is *
often the group design. In its broadest sense, group design is the *
overall plan for the group which will include general, as well as *
more detailed specifications. Generally you must decide and *
indicate: **who**, the target population; **what**, the purpose—what *
you think or hope the group should accomplish; **where** and *
when it will meet; and **how** the purposes of the group can be *
accomplished. The "how" will involve you in selecting (or *
possibly, developing) and organizing specific, structured group *
learning activities. Facts you already know about learning— *
analysis of learning deficits, the use of observation, rehearsal, feedback and sequencing—are, of course, still useful.

This last aspect of design development, the "how," is the one which will be the focus of attention in this text. The reason is that usually decisions about the clients for whom groups are needed, the purpose the group will fulfill, where and when the group will meet, are managerial or administrative decisions. Depending upon the size or nature of your group, you may or, more probably, may not be involved.

But we are putting the emphasis here on designs as meaning the selection of an effective series or program of structured group activities. If you think of the previous discussion about Group Goals and Activities, you will not find it difficult to understand that each activity in the series must serve, in some way, to help achieve the desired outcome which, in its turn, supports the achievement of Goals which, in turn, fulfill the Purpose of the group. To put this as baldly as possible, if you are developing the design for a Job Search/Support Group it is very unlikely that you will include an activity on how to saddle a horse—although you might struggle a little more with a decision to include or not to include an assertiveness component, especially given that time is not unlimited. It is also doubtless clear that these activities, once selected, must be ordered or put into a series so that activities can be built on the ones that went before.

But the development and implementation of design has more subtle requirements which call upon your skill and knowledge as a group leader.

The group goes through many changes during its lifetime. Some of these changes are the result of the usual Stages of group development (to be discussed next) while others will be the result of the needs and interactions of any particular group. The design, although it assumes a certain predictability in the group—and therefore incorporates some constants—must be flexible enough to accommodate the various Stages of group development, the unique "personality" of the group and any other accidental or chance elements which might emerge. In practical terms, this means that when you, as the leader, are planning, you try to anticipate what might be needed and have some "fall-back" or back-up" activities on hand. A good leader, in fact, always has an alternative activity on hand. The whole issue is so important that it, too, has its own chapter. A resource book of tried-and-true structured learning activities will be supplied to you at the workshop, as well as some already-prepared Program Packages which you may implement immediately or, perhaps, with only very minor adjustments.

The subject is included because knowledge of design is essential: leader skills and group design are complementary and inseparable. Just as any map is only useful if the cartographer who designs it and the navigator who applies it are truly skilled, so any design is only useful if it reflects group needs and if also the leader has the skill to bring it to life. Having a solid, reliable design will free you to attend to member needs and roles and to group processes but it is essential that you understand how the Design was developed.

STAGES OF GROUP DEVELOPMENT

Employment counselling groups which will bear good results will not just happen. All kinds of group needs, including the needs for inclusion, control and trust, must be met. In your role as leader you must understand the problems groups commonly face during their evolution, the obstacles which normally arise at successive stages, and how the obstacles may impede the completion of activities and the achievement of group goals. As leader, your role is in some ways like that of a supervisor at a building site. Happily for the supervisor and for group leaders and, indeed, for all of us, every problem does not arise every day. The activities and problems involved in digging a foundation are not the same as those of putting in windows and pity the supervisor who thinks they are. It is not necessary to belabour this point but it is necessary to point out that the leader works with the group to solve the problems, settle the issues and accomplish the tasks characteristic of successive developmental stages. Successful passage through each stage will bring both you and the group face to face with the problems and issues which result and which characterize the next stage. It will also bring you and the group closer to goal-achievement.

Tuckman et al (1965) have studied the developmental stages of well over 50 groups and their findings suggest that groups go through a predictable sequence of stages. Each stage builds upon the previous stage and has a purpose in helping the group move toward cohesion and high productivity. Figure 2 shows how these stages relate to the components introduced earlier. In this figure, the Stages of group development provide a third dimension to the model. Each stage will be elaborated fully in subsequent chapters. For now, a brief overview is presented to help you become orientated.

Figure 2:
Stages of Group Development

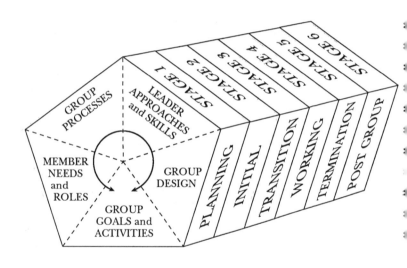

Another word of warning. We have used statements such as "The leader's skillful handling..." or, "At this stage the successful leader..." without describing what this skillful, successful leader does. You may feel you have missed something and ought to know these things already. Do not be alarmed, these skills will be described later. They are, after all, what the text is all about.

Stage I — Planning Stage

The main goal of the Planning Stage is to help the unemployed *
person understand the purposes of the group, that is, the specif- *
ic goals it seeks to accomplish. During the initial screening inter- *
view, the prospective group members must try to decide whether
joining the group will assist them to accomplish their goals, whatever they may be: job search, career exploration, etc. In other
words, prospective members must go through a process of
clarifying their own goals to see if there is a good match with the
goals of the proposed group. You, of course, play a part in
helping group members to arrive at a decision.

But before this "sifting" process, a great many operational
preparations must be made. Since CECs and the role of counsellors within them vary a great deal across the country, your involvement in the preparations may be large, small or inconse-
quential. It is necessary that you know what the preparations
should be and we are, therefore, for purposes of instruction, pro- *
ceeding on the assumption that you alone will take on the entire *
burden of preparing for the group—however unlikely this as- *
sumption may be in reality. Certainly with the manager of your *
CEC, and possibly your colleagues, you will discern a need, most *
likely in the form of a target population or a "set" of employment *
goals (assertiveness training, job search skills), assure yourself
that your colleagues understand what you have in mind, verify
the logistic, operational, clerical-support details, decide upon the
group design and do whatever else may be necessary to ensure a
good start and smooth functioning. Never be too proud to check
around to ensure a good set-up.

Stage II — Initial Stage

The principal focus, the major "happening" during the Initial *
Stage centres on the members' need for inclusion, to feel a part *
of the group. Simultaneously, members become acquainted, try *
to figure out their places in the group, define, if you like, their
relationship with other people. Everyone has done this. In a new
group we wonder (although maybe not explicitly): Whom do I

like? Not like? Should I line myself up with these people? Or those? Will they accept me? Like me? Am I going to be one of the standouts? Should I just hang back? Keep myself to myself *
until I see how things are? Members seek orientation to the *
group, its purposes and procedures. Corey (1982) says that the *
central issues for members cluster around the questions of trust *
and inclusion, whom they can trust and how much they can risk and self-disclose. In addition, norms are established which provide safety for the members and structure for the running of the group. Some norms result from the leader and group members working together: these are quite explicit. Others result from daily interaction. Members begin to figure out and learn what is expected of them, how to participate in the group and how the group will run.

During the Initial Stage, you must provide direction and work *
hard to promote member feelings of safety. In support of this *
aim, there is a focus on structured activities which build group cohesion. Remember that at this point, the members are just learning to interact with each other, although they are almost certainly not completely committed to the goals of the group or to each other. A good deal of dependence on the leader is characteristic of the Initial Stage.

Stage III — Transition Stage

During the Transition Stage, trust, very uncertain up to now, is slowly increasing and members slowly begin to assume responsibility for their own learning and behaviour as well as the learning and behaviour of the other members. Members are beginning to communicate more openly and risk-taking occurs more frequently. Underlying it all is the members' internal *
struggle to change, to overcome continued reluctance and *
uncertainty. In order to move the group forward, you will need *
to be both sensitive and encouraging when challenging members. You should always keep in mind that participants are engaged in this battle with their own discomfort about change—in addition to their fears and doubts that they will ever find a job—a lot to contend with. The behavioural responses *

resulting from this kind of doubt and anxiety will often be *
expressed in the form of dependence/ counterdependence (i.e., *
blowing hot and cold) in relation to you, the leader. Clearly, this *
sort of behavior, a kind of reluctance, will need skillful handling
by you. In the course of the Transition Stage, the dispersed and
hesitant energy and motivation of group members are har-
nessed, although often with some effort, to build an atmosphere
of safety, trust and universality. Universality refers to a perception that the feelings and ideas you believed were entirely and
peculiarly your own, occur also in other people, that other people share your problem and participate in the same fears. With
their anxiety mitigated, members should still maintain a sense of
individuality, independence and personal control. They will
begin to learn positive ways of resolving conflict and begin to
work at developing an attitude marked by acceptance and
tolerance toward themselves and toward other people. In this
more trusting atmosphere everyone feels safer about taking risks,
including, obviously, that of failure.

In the latter part of this stage, the group's norms and goals
are increasingly internalized by the members. What has happened is that members have integrated the principles and ideas
so thoroughly that they act upon them without having to give the
matter another thought. When this internalization has occurred,
members begin to monitor their own group's procedures. They
also develop a strong commitment to support and help each other. Conversely, individual group members now know they can
also count on the others for help and support. An atmosphere of
trust and commitment sets the stage to rally the group's resources to move on to the next, the Working Stage, optimally marked
by high productivity.

Remember that no stage arrives neatly encapsulated. With the *
Transition Stage particularly, it is the change which is character- *
istic. What is the case at the beginning, given that you make good *
use of your skills, is not the case at the end. *

One more thing. Sometimes the Transition Stage is pronounced. Often in structured learning groups it is so slight (and
so brief) that it is hardly apparent.

Stage IV — Working Stage

The Working Stage is characterized by intense commitment to *
the group's goals, high levels of task-focused activities and high *
levels of productivity. A marked degree of flexibility, problem *
solving, plus the ability to mediate and deal evenly and *
constructively with differences of opinion are characteristic of *
this stage. In fact, such differences of opinion at this point often *
provide rich and creative answers. The commitment to each
other, which was formed previously, continues and grows and so
does dedication to the task of job search. Johnson & Johnson,
(1982, p. 427) state:

> A definite sense of identity emerges—the group
> becomes a mature working unit possessing the skills
> and attitudes necessary for collaboration in maximiz-
> ing all members' learning...the group's attention
> alternates between task behaviour, maintaining clear
> communications...and working on keeping the quality
> of their relationship at a high level...there is a sense of
> pride in the group's work.

In order for the group to become productive, you help the members to learn the skills necessary to work with one another. There
is a change here from the Initial Stage where members tended to
depend on you–unavoidable at that point but not desirable in
the long run. At this Stage, ideally, members are interdependent,
relying on each other, having recourse to you only as you may be
needed for knowledge or information. Members see each other,
where once they saw only the leader, as sources of strength and
support and this development is very desirable. If members see
each other as source of strength, a corollary is that they sense the
strength within themselves as individuals.

Remember that this is also the Stage where the really purposive *
learning, the learning that has been designated as the group *
goals, the task-focused activities, take place.   *

Stage V — Termination Stage

The major effort at the Termination Stage is for the members to   *
integrate their learnings. In other words, the members try out   *
what they have learned in their job search and make further   *
plans. As involvement with the group (community, meaning, and   *
structure) is about to end, some members will need to deal with   *
their feelings of loss. There may be some mild "acting out:" peo-   *
ple staying away, coming late. Reverting to dependency on the   *
leader is extremely common. For integration to occur the group
members also need to evaluate their experience and the degree
to which they have attained their goals.

Your activities will involve helping members to clarify what has
been accomplished and to contract with them to work on change
after the group ends. You will also need to examine and evaluate
the success of the group content and process. Inevitably, your
own leadership comes under scrutiny as well.

Stage VI — The Post Group Stage

The Post Group Stage is also a time for consolidation of the new   *
learnings, to use the knowledge and skills learned in the group   *
in order to find and secure employment. From time to time, the   *
members may meet for continued support and to renew their   *
motivation in the struggle with unemployment. Individual coun-   *
selling may be necessary to facilitate further growth for a few   *
people.   *

You should conduct individual member follow-up, in some
cases arranging for further referral and promoting support net-
works for those individuals who still face unemployment.

The development of the group through the Stages should be
viewed in its entirety. If the group counselling program is well
designed and organized and you make careful use of your skills,
the group's evolution will be smooth and the outcome productive. If not, the group's development may be blocked. A more detailed description of each stage will be presented in subsequent
chapters.

POINTS TO REMEMBER

- **The five components which are involved in developing and running a group include: Group Goals and Activities; Member Needs and Roles; Group Process; Leader Approaches and Skills; and Design.** The group process component contains six sub-components: communication patterns, norm setting, decision making, confronting the problem, problem solving and conflict management.

- **There are six Stages of Group Development: Planning; Initial; Transition; Working; Termination and Post Group. The Components, mentioned above, are present through the evolution of these six Stages.**

POINTS TO PONDER

Compare your personal experience in groups (as a participant or leader) with the Components and Stages that have been defined in this chapter. Do a mental "walk through."

EXERCISES

1. Test your memory by filling in the diagram listed following.

2. Choose any two components and describe the relationship between them

3. While group development tends to be sequential, progress through the stages does not always proceed in a strictly step-wise fashion. Please comment, using an example.

4. Describe ways in which evolving group members' needs across the stages of group development influence their behaviour.

Chapter 4

Group Leadership:
Approaches and Skills

OVERVIEW

Five components of group employment counselling were presented in the previous chapter but as you are probably keenly
aware the key to running an effective CEC group is you, the leader. You will decide who the members will be, what work the
group will do and how the group will be run. Above all, you will
manage the group's processes: communication, norms, decision
making and so on—which are the "muscles that make the group
go."

This chapter looks at the leader—the qualities of the person—and the leadership roles necessary for group management.
Leadership has two major requirements: knowledge and compe-
tency in <u>leadership</u>, and skills and knowledge and comprehen-
sion of <u>design</u>. These requirements are multidimensional and
complementary. Both are necessary to achieve the specified program goals. This chapter presents information about how to run
a group, the next focuses on design and other leadership issues.

It may seem to you that the skills section in this chapter reads
somewhat like a dictionary, or, anyway, a glossary of terms. It is
necessary, however, that you become familiar with these ideas before proceeding further with the study of this subject.

We therefore bit the bullet and duly set forth each term comforting ourselves that, after all, many people enjoy reading dictionaries and at least some of the expressions will already be familiar. The principles and skills they denote will come alive for you in the "hands on" training to follow. For now, try to become as familiar as you can with the contents of this chapter.

OBJECTIVES

Upon successful completion of this chapter it is expected that the reader will be able to:

1. describe the qualities of an effective leader;

2. describe the necessary skills of leadership;

3. understand and describe how the leadership approach changes as the group moves through the stages of development;

4. describe ethical and training issues important to group leaders.

PERSONAL QUALITIES OF THE LEADER

The study of the group leader is of central importance because, group counselling, much more than individual counselling, is based on the dynamics of interaction. The group leader is the central and decisive influence in the group process. The group leader brings her/his values and standards to the group. Even more importantly, the leader brings a set of expectations of how the group should behave and what the group should achieve. Also, the leader's personality can have an impact in a positive or negative way on the climate, atmosphere and the implicit rules of the group.

What follows is a list of desirable leader qualities. You may find your breath taken away as you read it because the list is, indeed, daunting. The perfect group leader who possesses all these qualities in perfect proportion may not exist. If you think that you already are perfectly self-aware, tolerant, practise an al-ways-positive outlook, etc., this kind of self-image is much more worrying than the one that says perhaps you don't measure up. But these qualities are the ones we are all called upon to have and toward which the most experienced group leaders strive.

You do not have to do all this by sheer will-power. It is a fact that many of the skills and techniques to be studied are an ex-pression of these qualities. It is also a fact that experience—including experience in individual counselling—will help you to acquire these qualities. Experience will also convince you that these ideals are not something which are externally imposed but are a logical outgrowth of the good practice of group counselling.

Self-aware:

A high level of self awareness is important. You should be very   *
sensitive to your strengths, weaknesses, conflict areas, motiva-   *
tions, needs and goals, so that your personal needs do not inter-   *
fere with those of the members or the movement of the group.   *
You must invite trust and confidence in your leadership but it is hardly necessary to say that the invitation will not be accepted if you appear to be using the group for some obscure (or not so obscure) ends of your own.

So much will probably be obvious to you. Where one may, in leading groups, be very *un*-aware is in the question of the agen-da. You have made your design and have clearly in mind where the group should be at the end of the session and this may seem to you to be of commanding importance. But what should com-mand you even more is whether the group can or wants to follow the same agenda. People in counselling always digress a little and sometimes these digressions can be important to the learning of the group.

Tolerant:

Tolerance for differences and changes in group processes plus a   *
capacity to cope with some unknowns, enables you to respond   *
effectively to member needs and possible shifts in the direction   *
of group goals.   *

This is a variation of the sticking-to-the-agenda question. Just as every child does not attain full growth at the same time or is the same size when she or he does—and we all have tolerance for this fact—there is the same kind of unevenness in the ways groups function which simply does not arise in individual counselling. Ex-teachers will be familiar with this phenomenon. Human beings simply do display a great deal of variety but every one is important and is entitled to a little consideration and accommodation.

Positive Outlook:

Whether you mean to or not, whether you like it or not, you will serve as a model and your behaviour will have a corresponding impact on members. A positive outlook enhances motivation and problem-solving responses, increases a sense of group bonding and promotes trust and cohesiveness in the early stages of the group's life. Most importantly, a positive outlook promotes hope and renewed purpose in the members.

You will understand, of course, that a positive outlook does not mean that you should behave like Pollyanna or deny real problems. (Or make maddening remarks like "Cheer up!" or "Don't worry!". When was the last time someone told you to "Cheer up!" and you did or "Don't worry!" and you didn't?) It *
does mean projecting a real confidence that ways will be found *
and problems can be solved. *

People-oriented:

A high-level of social interest and attention to group members by *
the leader tends to promote closer contact. This attitude also *
tends to build a climate of trust and reduces the level of defen- *
siveness in the group. (We assume that if you are not people- *
oriented, you would not be in counselling).

Involved and Concerned:

The way you speak, move and attend can convey warmth. When you are able to project this kind of warmth and caring you tend to promote feelings of acceptance and inclusion in members early on. The same attitude also establishes strong norms i.e., guidelines for member behaviour, of respect. *

*
*
*
*

There are groups where the leader is, by design, fairly passive, saying and interfering very little and allowing the personalities of the members to unfold and interact as they may. This sort of group and leader are perfectly acceptable for what they are doing but not for what you will be doing in groups within the CEC. You will be trained to work with structured learning activities, not to test where clients get into trouble but to help ensure they do not. You will need to be involved and concerned.

Empathic:

This characteristic involves an expressed understanding of other people's points of view with an attitude of genuineness and respect is essential if you are to convey understanding of the experiences of the members. It is also essential to the process, the development through communication, etc. In the group context, it brings about safety and trust. In all kinds of counselling, and in all kinds of human relationships, defenses melt like snow in July before the warmth of real empathy.

Open:

Openness conveys the fact that one is secure in one's own ideas and behaviour and that this security is accompanied by an attitude of acceptance toward the ideas of other people. This openness by the leader promotes a safe atmosphere for risk taking and self-disclosure by group members. *

*
*
*

What openness, being clear and certain about your ideas and non-defensive in relating to others, seems to convey is that there is very little danger in being oneself. Openness also projects an attitude of acceptance toward others. Your openness will promote a safe atmosphere for risk-taking and self-disclosure by group members. Of paramount importance is the fact that openness dispels any impression that you consider yourself in some way above it all—or above the clients.

Organized and Flexible:

Being able to design and run effective groups requires that a leader be both organized and flexible. You must understand the learning process and also have a good knowledge of what is involved in designing and planning structured learning activities. Planning is what requires you to be organized. Within this context, you must be willing and able to modify the design and activities to meet the needs of the group members—a necessity discussed earlier under the "Group Design" component.

In some ways, organization and flexibility are opposites. Organization and planning are completed ahead of time with a good deal of careful thought and they ensure that the group has direction. By contrast, it is in the nature of flexibility that it cannot be planned. Flexibility is an attitude that must be integrated by the leader—rather like designing a building to be earthquake-proof. When the earthquake comes, it is too late to start planning, so the building must be capable of spontaneous flexibility. While we hope there will be no earthquakes in your groups, there may be a few tremors. When this sort of thing happens, it is up to you, as leader, to respond in a flexible, confident manner.

But you still need the design and you need an agenda. They give purpose and direction to your actions. They also act as a point of reference and orientation when you must digress.

Up to this point we have been discussing qualities of the leader. Now let's look at what the leader does.

LEADERSHIP

You, as the leader, will function principally in two areas: in the practical use and application of **leader skills** and **activities** in relation to the group and to members, usually when the group is in session, and certainly in an interpersonal sense, and, secondly, in your knowledge and understanding of **design** and the way it relates to the achievement of group goals. Both activities are interdependent and affect the group's progress toward achieving its purpose. For instance, if you are good at leading but the design is poor, the group may not reach its goals although the members may enjoy themselves. On the other hand, if the design is good, but the leading is inadequate, the group will almost certainly not reach its goals and the members may be very unhappy. You, as the leader, must be skilled and knowledgeable in both areas.

Leading will be discussed in this chapter, along with issues about leading. Design is discussed in the next chapter.

LEADERSHIP APPROACH

An important question needs to be asked by potential leaders. "If members have developmental needs and groups evolve through predictable stages over time: How might I, as the leader, approach each stage? What do I do as the leader? And how do I do this?"

Reflect for a moment about a favourite group to which you belonged. Or to take a more obvious example, think of the difference in approach between the wonderful person who taught you Grade One and the more demanding individual who taught you high school Math. This difference in approach was brought about by the difference in your maturity.

Leadership "approach" refers to the "manner" in which the group is managed. The leadership approach is directly related to the needs of the members and the stage of development of the group. Thus, as the group matures and members become interdependent and responsible for the group's work, your approach will change to complement this development.

Groups often move through the initial, transition and working stages in a fairly smooth manner. Leadership approaches evolve from directing, influencing and facilitating according to this movement. It is important to note, however, that groups can evolve in a two step forward and one step backward fashion. A group may, for example, progress nicely through the Initial

Stage, spend very little time in Transition and begin to make real progress in the Working Stage. You then introduce an activity which, for whatever reason, makes members feel, once again, very uncertain. The group's needs may then catapult you back to a supportive and directive approach for half an hour or so.

Directing

As the group begins, you will find you need to work to initiate *
and promote interaction. These functions, and you may use *
structured activities which perform these functions, "get the ball rolling" by creating an environment which will help the members of the group understand what they can expect from each other and the group. This direction starts the members discussing pertinent issues with one another. Remember that in the Initial Stage group members want to feel included in the group. But as the group is at this time, you are the only person they know— their sole link—and they may display a great deal of dependency. Directing is needed when the group is low in maturity, as, for in- *
stance, when group members are unable or unsure of how to *
take responsibility for themselves in the group and, therefore, need you to give clear, specific directions from the leader. They may want an agenda written on the board while probably later they will not.

This leadership approach is characterized by one-way commu- *
nication in which you define the roles of group members and tell *
them how, when and where to do certain tasks. You will provide *
a great deal of structure, for example: "Break up into groups of four: Edward, Mustaphia, Regeanne and Davica, then June, Eloise,..." Later you will simply say: "Form into groups...". As the members experience more understanding of their roles and tasks, their motivation increases. This leadership approach is required for the Planning and Initial Stages and, frequently, also in the Termination Stage when members may again, be feeling uncertain.

Influencing

Influencing is most suited for low to moderate group maturity. *
Members who are unable but willing to assume more responsibility for themselves and the group goals still need "direction" from
you that tells them to stay with their tasks, but this need should
be met by persuasion, support and encouragement which will reinforce willingness and enthusiasm. This leadership approach is *
called influencing, because while you are still directing in task *
and role responsibilities, you will try to accomplish what you *
want less explicitly, encouraging and promoting two-way commu- *
nication to help the members buy into the group's goals and *
decision-making processes. *

As the group matures and group members start grappling
with issues important and troubling to them (such as lack of confidence in job search or lack of specific job search skills), you
may encounter some reluctance from members who, like all of
us, are ambivalent or have a hard time accepting the need to
change attitudes or behaviours. At this point, you will influence
the discussion by keeping it on relevant issues and enhancing
communication for the same reasons. You influence (rather than
direct) the discussion so that it is focused on specific barriers to
employment and to resolving conflicts—whatever is needed to
keep the group moving ahead. This style of leadership is most
likely to be needed at the beginning of the Transition Stage.
With this approach you use a support (empathic) statement plus
a directing statement: "I know that you have all had bad experiences around this question and it is painful to discuss but it is
also one of the reasons we are here. And we must try to deal with
it!" Or you may offer a choice, indicating which is yours: "If you
like, we could do (a) or (b); (b) would be a real help in achieving this goal." You might also provide support of the "I know you
can do it!" type at this point.

Facilitating

Facilitating is the leadership approach that is appropriate for *
moderate to high group maturity. In other words, the group *

members have the ability and knowledge to complete the tasks *
and to assume responsibility for themselves and others. The lead- *
er acts more, in this approach, to get things going: sharing the *
decision-making with the members initiating, facilitating, and ral- *
lying group resources to support member efforts. This leader- *
ship approach is more effective in the latter part of the Transi- *
tion Stage and the beginning of the Working Stage.   *

Delegating

Delegating is a leadership approach for a mature group in the
Working Stage which has the ability, knowledge, motivation and *
skills to change and complete the group's goal. Little direction is *
needed from you and the group members provide their own sup- *
port and structure. Group members have developed an intense *
commitment to the group and they can act as a resource to one
another in terms of encouragement, specific feedback in job
search, simulation exercises, challenges and so on. This leadership approach allows the group members considerable freedom
and autonomy in completing tasks. It is most effective in the *
Working Stage.   *

What has happened here is that members have actually taken
over some of the leader's roles. Where you earlier might have
given directions, they will, if they perceive the need, direct a fellow member: "Let me show you how to do that...", "What you
have to do when you do that is...". They will encourage and support each other, maybe challenge. "You know we all agreed it's
hard to own our problems so don't you try ducking out..." (Maybe a little more directly than you might do but that is the privi-
lege between peers!).

It is not so much, perhaps, that you delegate to them as that
they delegate you to a much less active (you will remain as a
resource person) part in what goes on. You still initiate the structured activities, but during the activities your role is more low
key.

As the Termination Stage begins, you will return to a more di- *
recting approach. Group members have a need, during this *
stage, for imposed leader structure and direction due to feelings *

of sadness and impending perceived loss (of meaning, structure *
and community). In a way, they are about to join a new group: *
everyone-out-there minus this group, and the prospect may produce or revive feelings of uncertainty.

During the Post-Group Stage, your approach is, again, both
directing and influencing, as you work to encourage members to
stick with the job search contracts and to use their newly acquired skills.

Figure 3 (p. 50) presents a view of the leadership approach in
relationship to the Group Stage Theory of Development which
has been adopted for this text. Study it keeping in mind our
words of caution about the unevenness of group development.

LEADERSHIP SKILLS

We have just discussed the leadership approaches you may use in
responding to the different needs the group may manifest. Now
we will set out to examine the skills you will need to put these approaches into effect.

Leadership skills can be divided into three major categories:
REACTION SKILLS, INTERACTION SKILLS, and **ACTION SKILLS**
(Trotzer, 1977). The Reaction skills are used to express understanding of the needs and actions of individuals and the group as
a whole. The leader utilizes Interaction skills to guide and stimu-
late group interaction. In addition, Action skills are necessary to
direct and promote the group processes. The specific skills in
each of these categories will be introduced and defined to provide an initial understanding of the range of leader skills you will
need to master.

Most of the skills which we will present you will recognize immediately—you learned them in Modules I and II. It is, however,
necessary to re-examine these skills within the context of group
counselling. There are a few additions, new skills that relate
directly to leading the group.

These skills are classified in the way we have indicated. They
do not unfortunately cluster themselves conveniently in other
ways so that we can say: "Here are the skills for each leadership

Figure 3: Leadership Approach in Relationship
to the Stages of Group Development

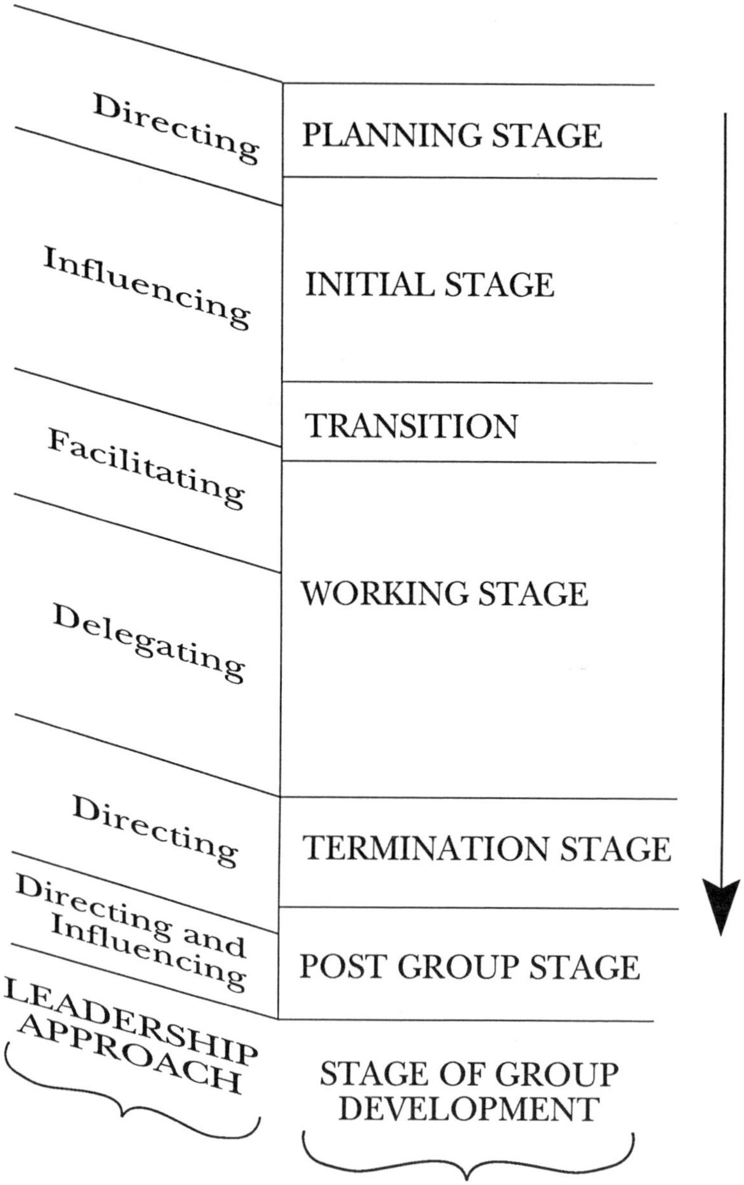

LEADERSHIP APPROACH	STAGE OF GROUP DEVELOPMENT
Directing	PLANNING STAGE
Influencing	INITIAL STAGE
Facilitating	TRANSITION
Delegating	WORKING STAGE
Directing	TERMINATION STAGE
Directing and Influencing	POST GROUP STAGE

approach, or for each Stage." You must use your knowledge, sensitivity and good sense in making an assessment and then selecting and using the appropriate skill.

Reaction Skills

These are the skills which are universal. They are used in individual counselling and you will continue to use them in one-on-one exchanges with clients within the group setting. You will notice also as this chapter continues that these skills may be used in support of some group skills.

Active Listening

Active listening forms the basis of much of counselling when it intends to say: I am listening, I hear what you are saying, I can see why you are special, I value your unique qualities, I understand. We all know that one of the most common problems in communication is failing to listen carefully to one another or to take the time to check what has been heard. Active listening includes attending to non-verbal messages (in the case of body language, this means listening with your eyes) as well as the words spoken. Well done, active listening provides a reliable data base which assists clear communication because it is drawn from observation of several kinds of behaviour: not just what was said but what was not, silence, laughter and body language.

Paraphrase

One way to ensure good listening is to check what you think was said or what you think you heard, with other group members. Compare your action here (paraphrase) your understanding of what the member has said and, of course, you do so with the same genuineness and respect for the member as you do when there is only one client present. Otherwise paraphrasing, as you know, becomes nothing more than a hollow echo. A hollow echo is annoying for a single client, in group, it takes on a ludicrous quality we all prefer to avoid.

Example:

Member: You seem like a nice bunch of people and I sure need a job but my mother has arthritis and she can't come and look after my baby every day. And like—sometimes I'm tired if he's been up all night—it's real hard to go out in the cold.

Leader: If I understand you correctly, you would like to continue in the group, but you're kind of telling everyone you don't think that you can promise to be here every day.

Clarifying

With even the best use of listening and restatement skills and, often, because of them, situations may arise when you will need to straighten out confusing or unclear aspects of a message. Sometimes you can achieve this kind of clarification by simply asking for a repetition, at other times you may have to request additional details.

Example:

Member: It's different looking for work here than looking for work on my own...

Leader: Different? I am not clear what different means?

Member: There are more people.

Leader: How does that change things?

Member: Like they help you and you help them. I don't feel lonely.

Empathy

According to Egan (1985), empathy involves the accurate understanding of another person's point of view coupled with a clear communication of that understanding. It requires the use of active listening and restatement or clarifying (reflection of feelings and content) in a manner that lets the other person know that you have clearly understood the meaning of his/her verbal message, voice tone, and non-verbal behaviour: the sensitive sum total of your active listening. Empathy also requires that you suspend critical judgment about what has been said and respond according to what the member perceives the experience to be. In particular, you are called upon to reflect accurately feelings along with the experiences and behaviours that may accompany those feelings. You should respond this way even when the member's perception is at odds with your own.

Example:

Member: You see this place and you think: Maybe they'll have something for me! Then you go in and ask and they say: Sorry! We're not hiring! Why the hell do I ask?

Leader: You feel really frustrated with the number of times you have been told that you won't be hired. You get mad at yourself for even hoping!

Summarizing

At several points in a discussion you will need to pull together and summarize the important aspects of the communication. This action can serve as a conclusion, and, as you know, an important means of transition from one topic to another. In the group context, summarizing pulls together several members' contributions. It helps to organize and integrate information arising from use of all the other reactive skills as well as discussions and it encourages progress in a more focused way. It should be used frequently, as it promotes movement.

Example:

Leader: Hey! Hey! This is a lot of information! Everyone's goals are a little different, that's clear. It seems to me there are some that really stand out. Let's see if this is what this group wants to accomplish.

Example:

Leader: A number of good points have been made about how to
set up a resumé. Let's take a few moments to go over
them and write them on the flip chart.

Example:

Leader: So we've had a good discussion about sweaty palms and
not knowing what to say and a few other things that can
go wrong when you are looking for a job. Perhaps we
should take time to make a list of what worries people
most—or most often. From these, we might decide what
really needs work.

Information Giving

You will be the source of specific information which might be
needed. In the group context leaders must be prepared to give
this information, when appropriate (that is: when it is requested
or when you perceived the need) in a clear, non-threatening,
and succinct fashion. You should also be able to advise people
how to obtain additional details.

Example:

Leader: I would like to share with you a list of the points that employers consider important in making a good impres-
sion in an interview.

INTERACTION SKILLS

These represent the heart of the group skills which you will use
in promoting and guiding interaction. They relate in large part
to the processes (communication, decision-making, etc.) which
are the "muscle" of the group.

Moderating

In using this skill, the group leader works to ensure that all sides of an issue are heard when there seems to be a strong "group" desire to go one way or another. What you will be moderating, or trying to keep within bounds, is a general movement in the group, perhaps a decision taken with much enthusiasm, which seems very strong but which, you fear, may not have everyone's support. In every group, some members hesitate to share their points of view. You must be sensitive to this hesitation and encourage their participation. Sensitivity means watching out for hesitaters. Since they do not speak, you need to keep an eye on body language and when they laugh—or do not laugh, etc. You may have to persist. Habitual hangers-back may find it difficult to believe that anyone really cares about their input and may quickly get into a hindering role.

Example:

Leader: A number of people have mentioned their interest in spending more time practicing telephone techniques. I am sure that everyone would agree with this change in focus. Mary and John, you haven't spoken about this. Maybe you can tell us what you think.

Example:

Leader: We don't seem to be getting anywhere today. We were going to begin practice with the video this morning. I am wondering to what extent the lack of progress might be a reflection of an uneasiness about this new task. Could I have some reactions from you about this?

Example:

Leader: I can't help noticing! A couple of days ago, you were all working independently—nobody needed me. Today, everyone's acting as if I am the only person who knows anything. I am wondering if you are feeling a little panicky because this is our next-to-last session. Can anyone tell me how they're feeling this morning?

Linking

As you listen to the various points in a discussion you may sense a need to draw some of the ideas together and point out the similarities—or "link" the ideas. Linking serves to develop cohesiveness and helps to diminish some of the apparent differences among group members. Often, two members of a group may be saying the same thing, but be using slightly different terminology in relaying their messages. This is a skill which builds cohesion quickly.

Example:

Leader: Although you and Judy seem to be coming down on different sides of this issue, I am not sure that you are as far apart as you think. You both agree on the importance of highlighting functional skills on the resumé. Your major difference seems to be whether these should be rank ordered.

Example:

Leader: Jack says every time he's turned down for a job, he feels like crawling away to die. Paul says that's terrible—he thinks you should never give in. They sound different but they're talking about the same thing: being turned down hurts!

Example:

Leader: Maria says she is uncomfortable about filling in forms and Anek says he never knows what sort of answers to give in the interviews. It seems to me that what we have here is an uncertainty about what employers are really looking for.

In this example there is certainly some Linking which will help to build group cohesion.

Blocking

Groups can be dysfunctional at certain times and you must be prepared to stop or block undesirable, unethical or inappropriate behaviour. People do not come to groups to be hurt and they will rely on you to prevent this from happening. There are times when members in small groups will scapegoat or turn on certain individuals and you must be firm in using your skills to prevent matters from becoming painful. Preventing situations from degenerating and getting worse is your responsibility.

Example:

Member: This is the third time that Jill has been late this week. If she wants to act like this she should just get out.

Members: (chorus of 'I agree')

Leader: Jill has been late on a number of occasions this week, however, I think we should wait to hear what she has to say before jumping to conclusions.

Supporting

In order to promote cohesiveness and productive action, you must offer encouragement and reinforcement to group members in their efforts to interact in the group. When people are recognized and supported in the group, they enjoy (and contribute to) an atmosphere of trust, openness and risk-taking. Shy members need to be encouraged to participate. Everyone should feel free to express their opinions. Shy people, to repeat, may need to be "liberated" by your support and recognition before they feel safe enough to participate.

Example:

Leader: Pierrette, I know you have a lot of trouble asking friends for job leads—and that's a kind of difficulty many people have and we'd all like to work on. Could you help us out by explaining the kinds of things that hold you back?

Example:

Leader: Madeleine, you don't say a lot but I know you're a whiz at finding your way around application forms. Would you share your secrets with us?

Note also, as the leader, you can support by reinforcing when shy members eventually do join in, by taking care to let them know you value their participation.

Example:

Leader: Thank you! That was most helpful. That was terrific. What you say makes a lot of sense.

Limiting

With this skill you define boundaries and set the limits within which the group will operate. In imposing limits, you establish a safe structure for interaction which protects the rights of group members.

Example:

Leader: It is important that we feel free to speak openly in the group. In order for this to happen we must be assured that what is discussed here does not get repeated outside the group. Can everyone agree not to talk about what happens here outside of this room?

Example:

Leader: In this group, people are going to practice skills and other people are going to give them feedback on how well they do. I expect some of you feel nervous about it. Here are the rules for giving feedback. If we stick to these rules, everyone can feel heard and understood.

Example:

Leader: As we talked, it seemed really clear that everyone is feeling very sensitive about being unemployed. No one is feeling wonderful about themselves and no one needs to feel worse. So I think there should be a rule right up front about no put-down remarks.

Consensus-taking

From time to time, the group leader must check out the perceptions of each and every group member with regard to particular topics or problems. Stop the discussion and have each person indicate his or her views, preference, where she or he stands. This is different from Moderating where you actually seek out people who have said nothing in order to achieve balance. Consensus-taking if often simply a regular "go-around". Topics of high emotional content need to be monitored through consensus.

Example:

Leader: There has been a lot of talk about extending the group for another three sessions. I am ready to see if this can be arranged. Before I do I want each one of you to indicate whether you would like to see another three sessions. John, would you start off? (Simply do a go

around to every member of the group. This action
ensures a valid consensus).

Example:

Leader: Now, I am going to go around the group and I want
each one of you to tell me, on a scale from one to seven,
how much you want to see this happen.

Note: Votes should be avoided—they tend to be divisive. People
often feel unreconciled after the voting.

ACTION SKILLS

As you have seen, Reactive skills involve the leader in attempting
to understand clearly issues presented by each group member.
Interactive skills call upon the leader to draw together themes in
statements made by group members and generally work with the
group as a whole. Action skills evolve from the first two and
require the leader to act by challenging group members'
perceptions of their issues and by helping them to develop and
practice more effective ways of dealing with their problems.

It is important to note that Action skills are not applied solely
in connection with employment issues (i.e., job search
strategies), but are equally applicable in helping group members
deal with emotional/additudinal issues (e.g., self confidence).

Questioning

Questioning is often overused in counselling, particularly the
closed questions which produce a yes-no answer. Questions are
useful and necessary. They should, however, be of a probing or
open-ended nature—the sort which help people to reflect more
and expand their thinking.

Example:

Leader: You have described some of the ways in which the interviewer was ill-prepared and asked inappropriate questions. Can you tell us more about your reactions in the interview so that we will all know better if that sort of thing should happen to anyone else?

Example:

Leader: Paul, you have a very definite attitude toward dealing with rejection. You just want to keep fighting back—lots of people, like Jack, just want to crawl away and die. Can you help our discussion by saying what contributes to the way that you feel?

Example:

Leader: Debbie, when you give feedback, you seem very, very reluctant to say what was wrong. Could you describe some of the things that hold you back? Maybe that way you can start to get rid of what is worrying you!

Advanced empathy

In using empathy skills, the leader becomes aware of the subjective world of a group member by monitoring non-verbal and verbal communication. With advanced empathy skills you focus on the aspects of this awareness which are not being acknowledged such as intentions, wishes, fears and needs. Sometimes these reasons are not recognized by the individual him or herself, sometimes people think that they ought not to have these feelings, intentions and so on. Advanced empathy can help group members rethink or reframe their attitudes towards issues facing them.

Example:

Leader: I get the sense that you are really angry about being out of work but you think you shouldn't be. This business of being a good sport must take up all your energy.

Example:

Leader: Catherine, you told us how you got specially dressed for this interview, got yourself all psyched up and really felt hopeful. Then when you got there, the employer couldn't see you. You're laughing and being a good sport but I am wondering if you also felt pretty mad and disappointed, and maybe had some of those panicky feelings about never getting a job again!

Confronting

If members indulge in behaviours which "block" the group, prevent other members from engaging in necessary activities, focus attention on themselves, or are in any way counter-productive, then the leader will need to confront the member with what is happening. Confronting is most effective after a foundation of trust and acceptance has been established. In fact, a leader who confronts before trust is established may be perceived as critical, hostile, aggressive or punishing.

Handle with care! Confronting is not an easy skill. It is best done, as you will know, when a relationship is established. With one client you may gently confront with the discrepancy between what the individual is saying and what he or she is doing, to give the most obvious example. In a private situation where trust exists, the client will usually not feel threatened and there is a good possibility that the confrontation will go smoothly.

It will be immediately clear to you that the situation in a group will require great sensitivity. Trust, as we have said, must already be established. The difficulty here is not simply that the individual is impeding his or her progress by failing to perceive an inconsistency. The difficulty is that this person is impeding the progress of the group by a particular behaviour. What follows is a very brief "formula" for confronting in the group setting. There are two principles which it is critical for you to keep in mind while applying it: There is a very good reason for this behaviour (fear and anger, for example) and it is the behaviour, not the individual, which is under discussion. In confronting: first, make an accurate, empathic response, second, address the specific behaviour and third, invite the member to respond or "dialogue" with you.

Example:

Leader: You're a lot of fun, Madeleine, and we all enjoy your jokes. They're a big help when so many people are feeling kind of down. But we've got to do some work and stop kidding around or they're never going to feel anything else. Is it OK to move on?

Example:

Leader: Barry, you're really enthusiastic! But I do think you've got your interviewing skills down pat and don't need to practice them any more—even though I sense you want to perfect them to insure you won't blow it. I'm wondering if it's possible for us to move on to some of the other group members now?

Obviously, it is important to be able to juxtapose the need for this confrontation with the ability to recognize that, in this case, Barry may actually have needed some extra attention. Also, you have the responsibility to make sure everyone has a fair chance to practice.

Immediacy

Immediacy is the skill of bringing into the open the dynamics underlying communication between the leader and group members. With this skill the leader is aware of the way communication is taking place at different levels and is committed to dealing with such discrepancies as may occur in an open and honest fashion. A here-and-now immediacy statement is most useful in the group context. It helps members to reframe, that is, view what has been happening in the group from a different perspective.

Example:

Leader: I am trying to give you some feedback on your resumé, but I sense that you are not really ready to listen to what I have to say. I wonder if our disagreement this morning is throwing up some interference.

Example:

Leader: George, it's great to be a good sport about the way you accept feedback. But you seem frequently to agree too hard with all the bad stuff. "Yes, I know I did badly, I am awful at this stuff." Martha, what do you feel like when you give George feedback and he puts himself down like that?

Martha: I feel like I just hit him! Maybe I am too mean and I ought to lay off. I wonder if he's afraid he can't improve and he wants us to get off his back? Because really he's good at this interviewing.

Leader: Is that what's happening, George?

Example:

Leader: Lil, I don't think Anita heard you. She looks sad and withdrawn. Can you think of another way to say what you mean?

A Quintessential Example of Immediacy

Leader: You have a good point but the way you said it made me feel terrible.

Immediacy is also a type of confronting: in both cases, you want the group member to take a good look at what is happening. The difference is that with immediacy what is being discussed are the feelings between people "right now." Again, always finish an immediacy statement with an invitation to look at it. It is very important to be clear that it is not the individual who is at fault. It is not even the anger, embarrassment or whatever. The member is entitled to his or her emotions. What is important is that the behaviour and the emotions it provokes are making problems. By the use of immediacy, you make an opportunity to set things straight.

Self-disclosure

Sometimes it can be helpful to the progress of the group to disclose something of yourself: a past experience, an emotion. In making disclosures you must be genuine and sensitive to the amount and depth of personal revelation appropriate for the group. You will use this skill in order to form bonds of trust and acceptance with the group members, promote cohesiveness and mutuality, and facilitate movement when the group or an individual blocks or gets stuck.

Example:

Leader: Now that we are on the topic of cutting resumés down to size, I should show you what I concocted when I first started looking for a job. Actually it's more of a small essay than a resumé. It didn't take me long to realize that this just wasn't working.

Example:

Leader: I can sympathize because I used to tie myself up in knots about dealing with this kind of person, too. Once I understood they were as worried and uncertain as I was, I seemed to be able to move right ahead.

Self-disclosure can be an excellent way for a leader to project empathy of the "I've been there" variety. Obviously, it must be used with care. You do not want to go on so long that the group gets the impression that not only have you been there but that you are stuck there. Self-disclosure can also be a powerful way of projecting genuineness.

Example:

Leader: That part always worried me, too... But when I saw how important it is, I decided to put up with the worry and just push on!

These sorts of remarks show you have some of the same emotions as other people and feel no constraint to hide them. Self-disclosure is, therefore, a close relative of openness. You are more real and, therefore, more credible.

Modelling

The very fact that you are the leader means that you are the focus of attention and set an example of acceptable behaviour inside and outside of the group. (See the previous discussion under "Positive Outlook" in the section on "Personal Qualities of the Leader"). Group members will acquire a good deal of information about methods of communication and desirable personal qualities from watching you. Members will often take their cues from you and change their own behaviour and involvement accordingly.

Example:

Leader: Today we are going to practise telephone techniques in approaching employers. I wonder, Sonja, if you would mind playing the role of a potential employer? And I will be a person seeking employment.

This is a very clear example: you are actually going to show people what to do. You probably do some modelling of this sort in individual counselling in order to provide an opportunity for a client to observe in order to learn.

You also model attitudes in a less explicit way. If you remember Jill (in the Blocking example) who was always late, you might imagine that the leader might have said:

Leader: I find it upsetting that Jill is late so often. But I think we should wait to hear what she has to say before jumping to conclusions.

You will note that this example now includes an element of Self-disclosure. The leader is modelling that it is O.K. to have negative feelings: impatience, annoyance, etc., but it is also possible to balance them with a sense of fairness.

As the group progresses and members begin to take over some of the leadership tasks, they will also begin to model and accept each other as models, accepting and valuing individual differences even, it is to be hoped, when these occur in themselves!

Process Observing

You need not only be aware of individual group members, but also be cognizant of the dynamics of the group. You must be aware of what is happening in the group and what type of interventions are appropriate at various stages. While this monitoring process is often internal, your observations may sometimes be profitably shared with the group as a whole. The members can then be involved in evaluating what is happening and discuss the implications for further action.

Example:

Leader: During this last practice session I really became aware that we have come a long way in terms of giving one another honest and direct feedback. We seem to be a lot more open with one another, what do you think?

Example:

Leader: I have been observing the group during this activity. At times you seemed to be bogged down or somewhat confused. If you would ask for clarification when you're not sure what other people are saying, it would probably help a lot more people than just yourself—and more people could get on with the tasks.

The leader, by use of Process Observation and, possibly, later by the use of Linking helps everyone to work more effectively on the task. Both these examples typify a way of observing the group process. You will note that the the statements make use of Immediacy.

Goal-setting/contracting

The establishment of concrete and achievable goals is a task that the group leader must assist individual group members and the group as a whole to address. One of the means by which this agreement is accomplished where it seems helpful is through contracting which you will recall from Module II. This is an approach which generally makes use of a written contract specifying goals, evaluation and rewards. It will be discussed in greater detail later in the book.

Example:

Leader: Everyone has the basic goal of getting a job, but I wonder if we can't break this big, general goal down into more concrete objectives. Let's start with job search, make a list of the parts of job search each of you would like to conquer.

LEADER ISSUES

In designing and running groups, you will face a variety of issues and decisions which must be made.

Two issues are basic to all group practice: these are to do with ethics and with training.

Ethical Issues

Ethical issues are a matter of high importance for all of us who may be in positions of trust. Some of these issues are particularly important in the group setting.

1. *Involuntary Membership*

CEC groups for unemployed people should be voluntary. The *
members must want something from the group. Efforts need to *
be directed toward clarifying issues and stating goals so that each *
individual can make an informed choice to join or not to join a *
CEC group. Each individual member can then decide his/her *
level of involvement. For this reason, a pre-group interview between the leader and potential group members is essential and far from a waste of time. It is also vital that you ensure that colleagues understand the nature of your work.

It is hardly necessary to say that forcing people to attend is unhelpful. Short of physical force, threats or blackmail there is no way that even the best leader can force someone to learn.

2. *Member and Leader Commitment and Responsibility*

Trotzer (1977) states that:

leader responsibility is an issue on a continuum, with one extreme stressing the leader as totally responsible for all the interaction and impact of the group and the other extreme placing the responsibility totally on the group with the leader sharing equal responsibility with the other group members (p. 91)

The authors agree with Mahler's (1969) position which states that "the main responsibility for growth of the group rests with members but the leader does all he/she can do facilitate that process" (p. 194). The leader, at all times, guarantees the * well-being of the members and ensures that group interactions * are constructive. Members have a right to assume that insofar as * possible, you will not allow them to be hurt but they must decide * their own level of commitment to goals and challenges. It is use- * ful to remember that the level of commitment will change as trust and cohesiveness grow.

3. Participation

Participation is encouraged but never forced on a group * member. At all times, each person must choose whether to * participate or hold back. Either way this decision holds risks * because the forces and influences in the group are powerful. You must attempt to reduce risks and hazards while simultaneously challenging and encouraging each individual to participate. The personal issues related to being a group member, which may cause some uncertainty, need to be discussed early on in the life of the group and group norms must be established to protect against potential risks. The risks around self-disclosure need to be discussed. Firm guidelines for feedback are a must. In a group where no one knows anyone, it is only human to worry that feedback may be painful. To a large degree, member participation in the group correlates with member "safety" in the group.

As leader you should, of course, also encourage participation by use of the Supporting Skill described earlier in this chapter.

On some rare occasions a group member may experience a crisis precipitated by an outside force. This individual may need one to one counselling support.

4. Confidentiality

Confidentiality is extremely important, the backbone of trust and self-disclosure. In a group setting, it is more difficult to secure confidentiality than it is in individual counselling. Member silence, an agreement not to disclose what occurs in the group to the outside environment, is of paramount importance to ensure that members feel safe. With a lack of confidentiality, the group morale and climate of trust will crumble, no wonder, the group is now a danger zone. You must not be afraid to repeat the need for confidentiality and if any breach occurs, deal with it firmly, quickly and openly. But the rule about confidentiality is modified in cases of significant danger. The Canadian Guidance and Counselling Association (CGCA) Guidelines for Ethical Behaviour (1981), are as follows (we have substituted "counsellor" for "members"):

> When a [counsellor] learns through a counselling relationship of conditions which are likely to harm others, the [counsellor] is expected to report the condition to an appropriate responsible authority. If the information has been received in confidence, the [counsellor] reveals the identity of the counsellee only when there is clear and imminent danger to an individual or to society and then only to an appropriate professional worker or public authority.
>
> If counsellees indicate that they are intending to harm themselves, then the [counsellor] is expected to take direct personal action to inform responsible authorities. The [counsellor] should consult with other professionals and should only assume responsibility for the counsellee's action after careful deliberation.

In other words, if a member confides that he or she is the one who has been planting bombs in local shopping centres, it would be less ethical for you to conceal this fact from the local authorities than it would be to betray the confidences of the member. And considerations of confidentiality do not predominate over considerations of physical safety. You clearly would not stand by and let people harm themselves rather than break confidence.

5. *Leader Values*

The leader's values do influence the manner in which a group is lead. Being aware of your individual value structure and the subtle ways these values may influence group members is an important ethical responsibility. Simply stated, you should challenge *

members to discover what is important for themselves. Do not try *
to persuade them to do what you, the leader, do or what other *
group members say is important and/or right.   *

Training of the Group Leaders

A group leader must have both a well-grounded knowledge of, *
and training in group counselling in order to be both competent *
and responsible. You should, naturally, only provide leadership *
for those groups for which you have specific training. If you are *
asked, you have a professional responsibility to represent your
credentials accurately. Professional responsibility extends also to
the need for continual upgrading of your skills and knowledge.

 The purpose of this initial part of Module III, Group
Employment Counselling, is to provide training and experience
in group design and leadership. The applied leadership training
will commence after the study of this book. CEC counsellors who
are concerned that they perhaps lack specific university training,
as such, should bear in mind that they have been trained already
in Modules I and II. The training to be provided in the workshop
for Module III will surpass the professional standards required
for minimal competence as a group leader.

POINTS TO REMEMBER

In order to help group members in a significant way, the leader
needs to possess leadership skills, understand groups and be prepared to work hard. The leader is the key to a successful group.

 Four major aspects of leading groups have been discussed.

  • **The leader must be someone who instills confidence by
  striving to possess and demonstrate desirable personal
  qualities (these qualities have been described);**

- the leadership approach must be adapted to the changing maturity and the fluctuating needs of the group;

- the leader uses specific, identifiable skills in guiding and helping the group;

- the observance of ethical group practice and the completion of adequate training are also central to honest group leadership.

POINTS TO PONDER

1. Think about the leadership qualities you possess. Decide in which ways you want to challenge yourself during the training. Prepare a contract with yourself to bring with you to training.

2. If you are a member of a leader-led group, observe the leadership approach (approaches) and use of skills as they may relate to the descriptions and discussions in this chapter. Try to evaluate how successful these approaches and skills are, i.e. a small "evaluation". Bring your observations to the training for further discussion.

3. Can you think of any leadership issues (ethics, purpose, training) that may be difficult for you to deal with in your particular CEC setting?

EXERCISES

1. Describe what you consider to be three important leader characteristics.

2. Listed below are a series of leader statements. For each statement indicate which particular skill(s) are being utilized.

(a) Leader: Now that we have had a chance to see everyone in action, let's divide into groups and give one another feedback. Before you begin, remember the role play and the discussion about giving feedback to one another.

Skill ?

(b) Leader: I can't quite understand what you mean when you say, "It's just too hard." What exactly do you mean by that?

Skill ?

(c) Leader: I don't think it's really fair to laugh at one another when mistakes are made. Jo-Anne, how did you feel when Peter started laughing?

Skill ?

(d) Leader: I know that this group has a lot of good ideas, but we are going to have to work at saying them one at a time if we are to benefit from them.

Skill ?

(e) Leader: Fred made a good point and Steve added an interesting twist. Does anyone have anything else to add?

Skill ?

(f) Leader: I can see from this situation and others today that we need to "re" practice our feedback skills. I know you don't want to hurt anyone's feelings. I think, however, there's a way to give feedback without being destructive. By not saying the necessary feedback we aren't really helping anyone move closer to their goal.

Skill?

(g) Leader: Perhaps we need to spend some time deciding what we want to do with our time today. This is the last session and I want to make sure that everyone's questions have been answered.

Skill ?

(h) Leader: I really must tell you how much I am enjoying this group. This is the first group of this type that I have run and I didn't know what to expect.

Skill?

(i) Leader: I know you're enthusiastic. Interrupting will create frustration and/or anger. It would be more effective to wait until others have finished speaking.

Skill ?

3. In the following two descriptions of a group interaction out line:

(a) which particular skills are being utilized positively by the leader,

and

(b) which particular skills are being violated by the leader.
  (i) John, a group member, has just finished role playing a job interview with Mary, the leader. He has done well, but has made a few glaring mistakes. In the debriefing session, a number of group members applaud John's efforts and describe some of the highlights of the interview. Mary writes the positive points on a flip chart and shows how these comments related to the guidebook in interviewing. As the discussion continues one of the group members brings up a criticism of how

John handled some of the questions. As a response, Mary makes the following statement, "We are not here to criticize one another, we need to support and encourage one another." This brings the discussion to a close and group moves to another activity.

Responses: a) ...b) ...

(ii) The group members have identified a number of barriers they are facing in finding work. The group leader, Henry, has initiated this activity and in the discussion the members emphasize only the differences among the barriers. Henry stops the group at this point and indicates that although there certainly are differences there also are similarities. He gives some examples and then looks at his watch and notices that it is time to stop. In the afternoon he moves to a new activity with a different focus.

Responses: a)... b)...

4. Compare effective leadership approaches often needed in the Initial stage with those most often needed in the Working stage of group development.

5. Assume you are starting your first group. Describe two ethical issues that you would need to take into account in working with colleagues and group members.

Chapter 5

Design

This chapter continues to discuss the leader and leadership responsibilities. As you will recall, the leader's impact on the group's ongoing interactions is related to the leader's personal qualities, approach and use of skills. Another very important way you will influence the group is through the program design, whether you develop it from scratch or (more probable) select one already prepared. This chapter will look in more depth at your responsibility in terms of design.

All design requires that the end result be accurately in the mind of the designer. Architects must know whether they are undertaking to build a theatre or an hotel, the playright undertakes to write a comedy or a tragedy, the potter will make a bowl or a teapot. You, in selecting (and, possibly modifying) a design for your group, know what is needed, what you hope to accomplish, the purpose of the group, what you want the members to know or be able to do at the end of the sessions. And just as any designer understands the medium; brick, plaster, glass and so on, you will understand yours: people in groups, how groups function, the stages they go through. Understanding, in this case, includes a knowledge of how adults learn (which might very well include the kind of observation, practice, feedback sequence used in Module II) and how they learn and behave in groups. Knowledge of how adults learn in groups (leaving aside considerations of how the group may help, the supportive environment it constitutes), for example, would also include knowledge of group stages, so that one consideration might be that whatever must be learned should require little risk at the beginning and increasing risk as trust builds.

Design obviously needs careful thought and, just as obviously, happens before the group starts and is necessarily an integral part of the Planning Stage. Do please note that it is a part, only, of the Planning Stage which also includes a great many purely operational considerations, notably a decision about the sort of group which will be useful to your CEC. The prime operational consideration, of course, is whether your manager wants you to establish and run such a group.

The Planning Stage requires your knowledge of the goals of the Commission and how it functions—the sort of general knowledge and perception possessed by any conscientious officer. You know the Commission wants clients to find employment; you know, almost by osmosis, why people do not find employment; you can spot a particular sub-grouping of such people within your CEC. You are familiar with the operational implications of running a group and the operational requirements of your CEC.

The Design, which we will discuss here, requires much more specialized knowledge and training: the careful exercise of everything that is learned in counselling and in the training in this module. You and/or your manager may, as we have seen, have noted a "clustering" of clients for whom it would be operationally desirable to set up a group and neither of you needs training to discern this fact. You do need special knowledge to know whether these people can be helped in a group, what you may reasonably hope to achieve and how you will achieve it. Design is the part of the Planning Stage which is done after all the administrative and operational elements have been nailed down, when you have the go ahead to establish your group.

The Planning Stage includes therefore, much more than the Design but the Design focuses and expresses the Planning Stage.

These two, the Planning Stage and the Design, certainly have elements in common, or to put it another way, you will find yourself thinking about the same kinds of matters whether you are planning or designing. At the end of the next chapter, the Planning Stage, we will indicate clearly how these two activities fit together. For now, simply for reasons of consistency, to finish off the components, we will study Design. We start with fundamental considerations.

A Note

Even though you will probably not, at least in the beginning, be required or expected to design entire group programs, it is vital that you understand how this process is undertaken. In the first place, Design is one of the essential Components of group. It has clear ties to the Group Goals and to the Leader Approaches and Skills you may use. It takes only a little thought to see that it will be implemented in tandem with the Group Processes and that it will be used to respond to Member Needs and that it is the ground on which Member Roles will be played out. For those of us who enjoy the actual practice of counselling: the interchange with clients, the use of inter-personal skills, the real satisfaction which comes from having provided real help, Design, which takes place in the absence of the client, may seem rather a cold business. Make no mistake: you perform no more caring or nurturing act than the selection (or, possibly, development) of a program Design which meets member needs and ensures that employment barriers are overcome.

It is probable that you will be provided with entire Program Packages which will outline every required activity in detail. Even so, you must examine the program in the light of a good knowledge of Design to assure yourself that every activity will be what the group needs. If it is not, you will want to substitute another but you must, in this case also, make a knowledgeable choice.

When you eventually come to implement the Design, it is necessary that you understand where each activity leads and what is required of you.

OBJECTIVES

Upon successful completion of this chapter it is expected that you will be competent to:

1. **describe the principles of learning in a structured group,**

2. **identify important broad issues that guide group design. and**

3. **identify the essential factors that need to be taken into account in developing a detailed plan for conducting a group.**

DESIGNING A STRUCTURED LEARNING PROGRAM

One of the most complex activities, then, that you, in your capacity as group leader, must understand is the method for developing a program, a series of structured activities, a learning experience which will allow a group to achieve its goals.

Design is the umbrella term for a cluster of activities which sets out the parameters of the group program, states the goals, describes, sequences, and develops the structured learning activities needed to achieve program goals. Design also includes organizing, and evaluating the group employment program.

Employment groups are structured learning groups. As you will recall from the introduction, a structured learning group focuses upon a specific subject matter—in this case gaining knowledge and skills for becoming employed and/or changing careers or overcoming other barriers to employment.

For adult learners, the structured learning situation with either a structured or a non-structured task, has certain advantages which non-structured situations do not possess. First and foremost is the de-emphasis, in the structured situation, upon the personality of the trainer or facilitator. The learning challenge is lodged in the situation itself, with the facilitating person less central within the boundaries of the constructed learning situation. This is not to imply that the facilitator need be less skilled nor less sensitive. Rather, it is he who constructs the situation (much work is done prior to the session), sets it in motion, and conducts the important processing period after the constructed situation has ended. Another feature of the structured learning situation is the psychological safety factor provided by the boundary of each structured situation. Since each situation is a complete entity, the consequences of one's way of being in one situation can end with that situation. Furthermore, the use of structure sets limits on the power of the leader, assuring the integrity of each individual's experience...(Middleman & Goldberg, 1972, p. 206–7).

Listed below are examples of "sets" of employment goals for which structured learning groups may be designed:

- assertiveness: preparing for employment
- reassessing options: changes in life directions
- career choice and decision-making
- job search/support

It is possible that, in the area served by the CEC in which you work, there exist employment barriers—implying, possibly, the need for a group to deal with these barriers—which are unique to your district.

Principles of Learning in the Structured Group

There are some principles which influence the design of any group, others apply particularly to structured groups.

1) The learner is actively involved in the learning   *
   experience as opposed to being a passive recipient.   *

2) The learning process has <u>intellectual</u> and <u>emotional</u>   *
   components.   *

3) The learners, by participating in selected learning   *
    activities, acquire insight into why and how they   *
    function in a group. Knowledge acquired through   *
    direct experience almost always has more impact than   *
    knowledge which is simply presented by others.   *

4) This awareness provides a basis and impetus for   *
    alternative ways of behaving. In order for real and   *
    lasting change to occur, a person's whole, cognitive-   *
    affective-behavioural system has to change. A   *
    behavioural change will be temporary without   *
    underlying attitudinal and cognitive change. It is   *
    possible, for example, to teach someone to smile during   *
    a job interview. The smile will be pretty vacant, however,   *
    if this person has no confidence or a mind set that the   *
    interviewer is always hostile.   *

5) The learning process is facilitated by a trained leader,   *
    you, and learning is achieved through a planned set of   *
    structured activities that build on previous knowledge   *
    and/or skills.   *

6) The more supportive and accepting the environment,   *
    the freer a person is to experiment with new behaviours   *
    and attitudes.   *

7) Change in a person's cognition, attitudes and behaviour   *
    is frequently better accomplished in the group context   *
    than it is in the individual context. The reason is that   *
    several comments of encouragement to a group   *
    member for a newly-acquired skill will be more   *
    reinforcing than a single comment.   *

8) A member's repertoire of behaviours is more likely to   *
    be expanded through participation in a group because   *
    a larger variety of behaviours will be modelled.   *

GUIDE FOR DESIGN

With any blueprint there are a number of markers which direct its development. In the case of planning for groups, these markers are called "guides." Four of these guides are listed below:

Program Goals

All design depends on what you want to do. Within the CEC setting, the Program Goals refer to the goal achievements which will eliminate or negate the identified employment barriers of a particular group of clients. Establishing the Program Goals *
represents the end of one part of the Planning Stage; for the *
designer, Program Goals represent the purpose, the leaping off *
point for Design. *

Stages of Group Development

Different stages pose different issues and suggest different *
activities. Knowledge of the impact of stage development on *
member behaviour shapes and directs the design. The specific *
relationship of each stage to design is outlined in subsequent chapters as each stage is described. An example of the type of structured activity suitable for the needs of the particular stage can also be found in each chapter.

Adaptability

The stages a group will pass through are predictable but the rhythm or pacing of the development can be uneven: each group falters or races at different points. As in all cases of navigating a course, frequently one must make adjustments and small detours. This also is the case in running a group. Hence, *
when developing a design, you anticipate possible variations in *
reactions and needs of the members. Optional structured *
activities should be included for substitution as the need arises. *
Pfieffer and Jones (1977) explain the need for flexibility by stating that:

There is no way that any group facilitation can anticipate all of the   *
responses of participants and all of the real-time concerns that   *
become relevant in producing a plan of activities for fostering   *
client learning. He/she needs to develop the ability to change   *
the learning design while the laboratory* is running. (p. 177).   *

Evaluation

Specific and explicit program goals and the objectives for each   *
session, in addition to their function in implying choice of   *
particular activities, form an excellent basis for defining the   *
measurement of outcomes–how you will know your group has   *
achieved the goals.   *

DEVELOPING THE DESIGN

By now you know the general purposes and goals of the group
and that they can be achieved across the stages of development.
You must also understand the need for flexibility and the way,
when the group finishes, you will evaluate your design in terms
of outcomes.

Keeping in mind the guides described, you can now begin to
flesh out the plan. This is best done in several steps. The steps
will be described fully and demonstrated during the leader
training sessions of the module. What follows is a summary.

1. *Operationalizing Goals*

In making goals operational the first question a leader asks him   *
or herself is: "What do I want my members to <u>know</u>, be able <u>to</u>   *
<u>do</u>, or <u>have experienced</u> by the end of the group or at particular   *
points during the life of the group?"   *

Think of the situation where you may want group members to
be able to perform well in a job interview. There are elements of
knowledge or understanding, there are elements of practical skill
and there are elements of emotion, feeling and attitude which all

---

* Note: Don't be put off by the word "laboratory." In this context
the authors are simply referring to a learning group.

go toward a good performance. At present there are deficiencies in all respects—or so you assume—and you must decide what exactly would constitute an indication that these deficiencies have been corrected.

Let's take a look at how goals might be operationalized:

KNOWLEDGE

The Deficiencies	*The Goals*
• Members do not know what employers are looking for or have in mind when they conduct an interview for a new employee;	• Members can describe or list the factors by which prospective employers will probably evaluate them, e.g. education, training, skills, experience, references and an assessment of their capacity to be effective, or a received impression of reliability;
• Members do not know what creates a good (or bad) impression;	• Members can describe the behaviour, e.g., punctuality, firm handshake, eye contact, "honest" clothes, which make a good impression;
• Members have no idea of how the employer is feeling during this interview;	• Members can describe some of the emotions and conflicts which employers experience around a job interview;
• Members do not know how long to stay or when to leave.	• Members can state appropriate lengths of time for an interview, describe employer behaviours which indicate the interview is at an end.

SKILLS

The Deficiencies	*The Goals*
• Members have limp handshake, do not make good eye contact, look scared;	• In simulated interview with three different group members, members can demonstrate firm handshake, eye contact, smile;
• Members stutter, stumble, make unclear replies, cannot describe their qualifications,	• Members can list, clearly and succinctly, their qualifications;
• Members cannot describe their good qualities;	• While making eye contact, members can describe appropriate experience, their good qualities, interest in this job, potential usefulness to employer;
• Members cannot respond appropriately to interviewer.	• Members describe their qualifications by responding appropriately to interviewer's questions, respond appropriately to general remarks by employer, initiate at least one (two, three, as you may decide) remarks which reflect well upon self.

EXPERIENCE

The Deficiencies	*The Goals*
• Members lack familiarity with the job interview "routine";	• Members become thoroughly familiar with the interview routine, through practice and simulation;
• Members are unable to imagine or understand what is in the mind of employers;	• Members have an experience as "the employer", can list two questions they thought important, list five job search behaviours they thought made a favourable impression;
• Members are uncertain of the image they project, when they "look good," when they don't;	• Members gain clear understanding of the image they project, what is good, what they wish to change, by means of videotape recall, can describe corrective actions they may take;
• Members "feel bad" about themselves and how they perform in interviews.	• Members feel increased confidence in their ability to go through a job interview, after practice, group support.

These skills needed to operationalize goals are clearly set out by Pfeiffer and Jones, (1973):

> The major set of skills relates to the ability to identify the learning goals of the training event very specifically. It cannot be stressed enough that laboratory* education is goal oriented, and it is important for the facilitator to learn ways to be able to clarify

---

* Note: There's that word again (laboratory). Remember that the authors are simply referring to a learning group.

his goals for a particular training event or a particular part of a training event, so that these are motivators for the particular learning experience itself. A closely related set of skills involves helping participants to clarify their own goals. It is important that human relations training activities be carried out in the light of highly specific goals that are related to the behaviour of participants. In designing a laboratory, then, one begins with establishing, in a highly specific way, the goals of the experience. (p.130)

As this quotation and the general orientation of this book, and, in fact, all counselling training indicates, member input into the establishment of goals is vital. You may suggest the necessity of understanding the interviewer, for example, when members do not. They will probably be grateful for your suggestion. But members will have very clear ideas of their own about what they have trouble saying or not saying or what exactly worries them in the job interview situation and your ability to be adaptable, will stand you in good stead.

2. *Time Frame*

Once you know what you are going to do, i.e., program goals have been stated, it is necessary to establish the time frame you have to run the program. (What is the total number of hours and/or days?) By identifying the time frames available, you are able to establish distinct blocks of times within which goals can be operationalized. It is really important that you do not undertake to have a group of clients achieve a set of goals which require more than you have. You may have to do some rigorous selection and weeding out when it comes to establishing goals and/or activities designed to achieve outcomes in the light of the time you have available.

The attention span of group members must also be taken into account when planning the length of the session and when determining pacing of activities in the group, e.g., a shorter attention span is usually characteristic of fifteen to seventeen year old adolescents, but every group has limits to the amount of time it can concentrate on one activity. You must plan for breaks and also allow for smaller, "taking a breather," breaks which will be more spontaneous.

3. *Determining the Setting*

Space, lighting, arranging for seating and room for people to *
move about are all factors which contribute, or fail to contribute, *
to an environment which is conductive to good learning. Limits *
on any of these factors may also inhibit your design: a small space, for example, will limit the effect of work in small groups because members wil obviously be able to overhear each other.

4. *Developing and Sequencing Structured Learning Activities*

By now it will be clear to you that the main method of facilitating member learning in employment counselling groups is through the development of specific learning activities. For the purposes of this program, the expression "structured learning activities" *
refers to any planned activity which intends that members *
acquire knowledge and skills for acting or reacting in particular *
situations and which constitute Operationalized Goals. Of *
course, you will want members to acquire these skills in company with an understanding of their own behaviour and that of others. This understanding is to be achieved by focusing attention on feelings and attitudes (see (4) Principles of Learning Structured Group).

The learning activities can have three major components: information, skill acquisition, and the examination of feelings, attitudes and beliefs to parallel the cognitive-affective-behavioural whole. The type of learning impact of various learning activities will be presented in detail in the training portion of this module. In the meantime, a useful guide can be found in the Table which follows.

Table I: Types of Training Activities Related to Training Goals

Training Goal	*Related Training Activities*
Knowledge and understanding	
Facts and information based on experience and research; generalizations or theory to facilitate application of learning.	Lectures, panels, reports. Reading and discussion of reading. Films, videotape recording. Group discussions, theory-building exercises, and knowledge tests.
Sensitivity	
Awareness of and empathy with other people's feelings, perceptions and attitudes.	Case Studies. Role playing and role reversal. Group discussions. Laboratory methods.
Self-insight	
Increasing self-awareness, understanding of own behaviour, and assessment of personal strengths and weaknesses.	Personal feedback. Use of video sound recordings. Role playing. Psychological tests. Personal counselling.
Attitudes	
Modifying biases and prejudices, freeing one's potential by reducing fears and other personal blocks.	Philosophical and personal discussion. Laboratory methods. Case study methods. Role playing and role reversal. Field experiences and inter-group activities. Films/Video tapes.

Skills

Learning new ways of behaving and implementing understandings; technical skills related to job developed through practice.	Skill training exercises. Practice experiences. Role playing. Demonstrations. Drill. Supervised practice.

The Series on Leadership and Group Development, Concordia University, Montreal, Dimock, 1973 (p. 14). (Table edited by authors).

Take a look at how you might work with the information in the table just presented. For purpose of illustration, we are going to work on the fact that members do not know how to make a good impression in an interview.

The Knowledge Goals:

Members can describe the behaviours, for example, punctuality, firm handshakes, eye-contact, which may be achieved by appropriate training activities. You might choose a mini-lecture or you may have a video of some employers describing the behaviours they prefer or you may choose a group discussion—whichever, in your judgment, will achieve the operationalized goal.

The Skills Goals:

Members can demonstrate firm handshake, make eye-contact. smile. You may decide to have first a demonstration followed by practice or drill.

Self-Insight Goals:

Members should know when they "look good" and when they don't. Perhaps you will decide to use video recordings to provide feedback.

The Attitudes Goals:

Members "feel bad" about themselves and how they perform in interviews. You might plan some discussion.

This kind of structured activity is suitable for the early stages of group development. The knowledge is easily acquired and so are the skills, which are those particularly, that can be practised in a routine, straightforward way. Responses requiring judgment, which have more risk involved, are not required. Feedback comes from a video so that, members may, as it were, make their mistakes in private. At the end, members have probably built up their self-confidence and their feelings of being comfortable and accepted in the group.

If you were planning a similar exercise for later on in the group's life, you might include role-playing, which requires more confidence or role-reversal, involving feedback from other, or another, group members. All these activities, while they imply good practice and the acquisition of more understanding and more complicated skills, also require more trust and a greater willingness to risk.

When descriptions of learning activities are included in the plan for the group, the following details must be included:

a) a title,

b) a clear indication of the developmental stage to which the exercise belongs and a statement of the goals the exercise is intended to support,

c) an explanation and a general outline of the way in which the exercise proceeds,

d) the number of members,

e) space and setting,

f) a list of all necessary materials (flip charts, pencils, etc.) and equipment, examples of forms, questionnaires,

g) any special materials needed,

h) an indication of total time needed:

i) a detailed, step-by-step account of the way in which the exercise is to proceed, including all explanations, directions, responses, etc. to be spoken by the leader, and including a description of each activity component, the objective of the component and the time required.

In designing plans for groups, you must set out the activities, * each one in relation to the other so that they form an integrated * whole. Essentially what this means is that after the activities have * been selected, the ordering of them is the next task. Pfieffer and * Jones (1977) explain sequencing as a part of the design process this way:

> Learning events are not put together in a random way; it is important that the facilitator be able to see the impact of one particular training component on the one which immediately follows it (p. 170).

In the development and sequencing of activity, you must consider how or in what ways the activity may be debriefed. Debriefing refers to the assessment of the impact of the activity on the individual and his/her goals. It promotes the integration of the knowledge and skills through increased awareness. The debriefing process involves the following:

1) sharing what happened: members saying what they felt about the activity;

2) processing what happened: members analyze and make sense out of it;

3) abstracting and generalizing what learning has take place; members indicate what they have learned;

4) application of the learning to individual and group goals: members examine the ways they would like to apply what they have learned.

"Debriefing" may sound like a cold process with faintly military overtones. In fact, it is a vital procedure for integrating the experience: What did I feel like? (Scared/successful/excited.);

What did this mean to me? (I was worrying for nothing/That was harder than I thought.); What did I learn? (I know more than I thought/Next time will be better.); How I can apply this information or skill to the learning goals? (I can write my resumé/Fill out forms correctly, etc.).

CHECKING THE DESIGN – A CONSUMER CHECK

Frequently you will discover that modification to the design can be easily made as a result of the knowledge gleaned from interviewing prospective members. Altering the plan to meet member goals and needs is a necessary form of flexibility. The pre-group interview, which doubles here as a User Check, and is also discussed in the next chapter, is another point where Design and Planning overlap.

In the remainder of the text, each chapter has a section entitled "Design", which describes the main issues of design for each stage of development. An illustration of an activity which has been developed utilizing the principles described above, is also included.

POINTS TO REMEMBER

- **Group design provides an overall blueprint for running a group as well as information regarding planning and sequencing of specific group activities.**

- **In using structured learning activities when developing a plan for an employment group, the leader must pay attention to:**

  a) how the activity fits the group's goals and,

  b) the sequence of the various activities.

Think about why these are two important considerations for establishing a group.

A POINT TO PONDER

In thinking about being organized but flexible in running a group, what will be the major challenges for you in keeping these two factors in balance?

EXERCISES

1. Based on your experience as an adult learner, and from the material in the text, describe what you consider to be three key principles of learning in a structured group.

2. This chapter describes four major issues in guiding the design of a group (program goals, stages of group development, adaptability, evaluation). Comment on the importance of each.

3. The essential factors in developing a design are described as—operationalizing goals, time frame, determining the setting and developing and sequencing structured learning activities. Describe the connection between goals and learning activities.

4. Decide upon a goal, operationalize it, select a developmental stage you judge would be accurate. Indicate a Knowledge, Skill and Self-Insight Goal and select an activity suitable both for acquisition of learning and the developmental stage you decided upon.

Chapter 6

Planning Stage

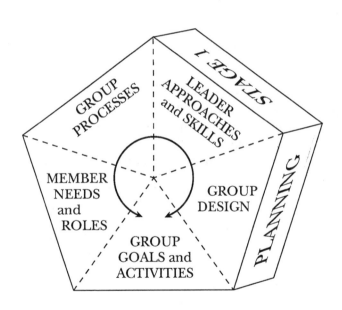

OVERVIEW

Planning for all groups starts with an idea, but the idea takes shape and becomes usable through consultation between you, supervisors, colleagues and clients. A great deal of planning is necessary before the group is launched and within a CEC (and, in fact, all organizations) planning is something which requires consultation with others.

The purpose of this chapter is to alert you to the essential matters which must be agreed to and decided upon before the group officially starts. Knowing what kind of group—The Purpose—is the obvious first step and from it all subsequent planning flows. But several other important tasks must be attended to before the group members assemble for the first time.

At this stage you will concentrate your efforts in the following areas:

- acquiring the approval of your manager and the cooperation and support of your colleagues, (equally, of course, you may act in response to a request which comes from your manager),
- checking and verifying all operational and administrative matters,
- ensuring that you have an appropriate design for your group, and
- recruiting members.

At the completion of this stage you will be ready to meet your group for the first time.

OBJECTIVES

Upon successful completion of this chapter, it is expected that you will be competent to:

1. **outline the basic rationale for the Planning Stage;**

2. **design an effective Needs Assessment;**

3. describe the necessity and advantages of developing a detailed proposal (purpose, objectives, practical considerations, procedures, evaluation methods) to obtain organizational approval;

4. describe the need for careful group member selection and list the criteria and methods used in making selections;

5. describe some of the challenges that a leader might face in the Planning Stage and outline strategies that can be used in meeting them.

CHARACTERISTICS OF THE PLANNING STAGE

Work in the Planning Stage has three major thrusts. The first is *
to establish the beachheads within the organization necessary to *
permit the formation and running of the group, the second is to *
ensure a design for the group which will lead to goal achieve- *
ment and the third is to screen prospective clients to ensure that *
the proposed group is suitable for the client and the client is suit- *
able for the group. *

Before taking even the first step toward planning a group, however, you need to ask yourself:

"Is this something that I am convinced should be done?"
(in the situation where you, rather than your manager, initiates group activities)
and
"Do I have the skill level to accomplish the desired results?"

Let us suppose that the answers to these questions are "yes". You should try to specify more precisely the target group and the underlying purpose or goals of the group, what you think it could/should accomplish, in short, the employment barriers to be overcome. To obtain this information, you may conduct a Needs Assessment, review existing literature, and examine relevant group employment materials in the field. Gathering this type of information will provide a foundation for the development of a detailed proposal, a necessary task which we will describe later in this chapter.

The point is that the proposal then becomes an effective tool for presenting ideas to colleagues and supervisors. Groups do not operate in a vacuum and you undoubtedly understand that it is in every way essential that support in general for the running of the group be obtained from CEC management. But more than is the case for individual counselling, group counselling requires support, formal and informal, from the entire Centre in which you work.

It is difficult, if not impossible to run a group successfully if your co-workers are not sold on the idea. Intentionally and unintentionally, skeptical colleagues will sabotage you, refer no clients or—just as bad—refer the wrong kind.* Your colleagues will not do these things to obstruct your progress, they will do them because they cannot in all fairness, be expected to refer clients to a program of which they have no understanding and in which they have no confidence. Take the time to explain how groups work and to deal with their fears. After all, a referral to your group is a referral of trust. Your co-workers may have had bad experiences: "The people in (another CEC) tried a group just last year. The guy who led it quit the Commission!" "My cousin's friend went to a group and he was depressed for three weeks after." These experiences were real, not imaginary. Colleagues may not want to "share" their clients, they may worry you intend to take over, even make them redundant.

Arguments and reason have their place. But it is most important that you deal with the anxiety and insecurity which underlie the "reasons." Do not be surprised if you are obliged to spend more time dealing with the apprehensions of colleagues than you do with the apprehensions of clients. The secret is to consult early and often. In this way, the proposed group becomes many people's project and has many people behind it.

---

* Note: This is a point made by Lawrence Shulman. "The reservations, negative reactions, fears and the like all come back to haunt the counsellor in the form of conscious or unconscious sabotage of the group." Shulman, Lawrence; Leading Employment Counselling Groups: A mutual aid approach, 1984, unpublished mimeo for the Employment Counselling Development Division, CEIC.

If insufficient attention is given to the Planning Stage, problems will emerge in the running of the group. The problems may be mildly irritating such as not having the required resources, or they can be more serious, such as having inappropriate people in the group. By taking the time in the beginning, you can avoid pitfalls and ensure that your ideas will translate themselves into an effective learning group.

We will now describe in detail how all this works, how planning should proceed.

NEEDS ASSESSMENT

In your particular employment office there may exist a limited group program or a vague awareness that some type of group counselling approach might be a "good thing". In order to establish more specifically what is needed, that is, frequently encountered employment barriers which must be overcome, you should begin by conducting a comprehensive needs assessment to obtain information from clients, colleagues and supervisors.

At this stage, the approach is still tentative, of the "asking around" type. In talking to supervisors and colleagues you should emphasize that all this discussion (the Needs Assessment) is simply a preliminary step to examine the need for a group counselling program.

While trying out your ideas you will naturally keep in mind the existing organizational policy and how it is being interpreted—don't waste time and effort in areas for which there is no mandate. You know CEIC policy better than we, the authors do, but just the same, we would like to remind you to keep this knowledge in mind and protect yourself from disappointment. Without question your supervisors and colleagues will help to keep you focused. All in all, you may reach a general consensus.

Next, you will need to gather data from clients, a step which requires approval and support from management. This is still an exploratory activity requiring minimal resource investment which should make it relatively easy to elicit the necessary support.

Once you have obtained basic support for the idea you should construct a short client questionnaire, then write a covering letter to explain to your colleagues what you have in mind.

In the situation where your manager or supervisor instructs you directly in the kind of group you are to run, you will still need to do a Needs Assessment. This procedure must always be   *
carried out because deciding upon the exact nature of the goals   *
to be achieved is, decidedly, the leader's task.   *

Example

(COVERING LETTER)

Dear Colleague: *
   *
I am checking to see the level of   *
interest among your clients in   *
becoming involved in a group   *
employment counselling program. I am   *
interested in running groups because   *
of my training and the benefits that   *
have been demonstrated through the   *
research literature. The exact nature   *
of the group will depend on the   *
response I get from clients through   *
you/your good offices.   *

Please distribute the attached survey   *
forms to clients who you think might   *
be suitable for a group counselling   *
program. If you have any questions or   *
comments, please do not hesitate to   *
contact me.   *

Sincerely,

Group Employment Counsellor

GROUP EMPLOYMENT SURVEY

All information you may supply us for this service will be treated
CONFIDENTIALLY. The purpose of the survey is to assess what *
types of counselling assistance would be helpful to our clients. In *
addition, the survey also addresses your interest in becoming in- *
volved in a group to work on various employment problems. *

1. Length of Unemployment *

2. Previous job *

3. What types of assistance would be helpful? Check as *
many as apply. *

a) financial planning ❑ *

b) career testing ❑ *

c) career exploration ❑ *

d) setting career goals ❑ *

e) job information ❑ *

f) job search skills ❑ *

g) support group ❑ *

h) others (please list)

4. If this CEC were to set up groups for 10-12 clients like *
yourself to provide assistance for any of the activities you *
have chosen (above), would you be interested in taking *
part? YES ❑ *
NO ❑ *

5. If you are interested in being considered for any special *
group programs that may be developed, please include *
your name, address, and telephone number so that we *
may contact you. *

6. Additional comments

The questionnaire should be distributed widely and the results tallied to provide some idea of the issues and interest in group counselling. In addition to gathering information in this way, which may be too "literary", or possibly, too much of a nuisance, for some clients, you may want to interview several clients about their needs and the group counselling option.

It is also important that co-workers be asked how many of their clients would benefit from a group employment counselling program. Again, by including co-workers and supervisors in preliminary discussions, you not only take advantage of their expertise, but also build a base for cooperation and support.

This is the time at which you will probably want, at least tentatively, to make a decision about the desired level of similarity among group members. The argument in favour of similar (homogeneous) groups is that members are of comparable age, sex, etc., and will be grappling with the same type of issues. In brief, they have a greater tendency to share the same point of view as well as the same barriers to employment. This kind of homogeneity is especially beneficial when the group is for clearly defined target populations: the handicapped, native peoples, immigrants, for example. Members of these groups are able to empathize with one another, have credibility, (adolescents tend to believe other adolescents, immigrants, other immigrants and so on) and are able to offer mutual support of a nature which is not possible for even the most talented group leader.

A general kind of bias in favour of demographically homogeneous groups exists: "We need a group for welfare recipients." "We should do a group for immigrants," etc. In point of fact, this kind of demographic designation is a short cut to saying: people in these groups share certain kinds of employment barriers. It is perfectly possible, however, for clients to be in different demographic groups, such as women returning to the work force and disadvantaged youth, and still to share an employment barrier, for example, the absence of a career choice or an incapacity to be appropriately assertive. Conversely, it is possible for people to be in the same demographic classification and have differing goals. Some refugees, for example, may need help with assertiveness and some with job search and you obviously would not want them in the same group. Goals then, rather than demographic characteristics, predominate in uniting the members of a group.

Probably you are thinking that you would do best to combine both: goals and demographic characteristics. There are certainly advantages to this plan. Providing members share goals, however, a great deal can be gained by mixing people of different backgrounds who are able to benefit from each other's experience.

Having decided upon the nature of group membership, you must determine how many people will be in the group and how they will be selected. The desired number of people in a group depends on the purpose for the group. If information giving is the major thrust, larger numbers can be accommodated. In most situations, however, it is desirable to keep the group size from 10 to 12 members. The complexity of a group is such that it is difficult for a leader to function effectively if the numbers increase much beyond 12 members.

ORGANIZATIONAL APPROVAL

Let us suppose that, by careful investigation, you have assessed the need and found it exists: you may have sensed the need then checked it out with your supervisor and colleagues *or* your manager may have sensed the need and instructed you to implement the group. Whichever the case, you should develop a detailed proposal.

Developing a proposal is an excellent means of getting your *
ideas firmed up and clarified: Will there be a "target" popula- *
tion? If not, what about the characteristics of the clients who will
be in the group? What do you hope to accomplish? How?
When? In organizational terms, the proposal is the means by
which you seek permission to go ahead whether you are seeking
permission or following instructions. The proposal shows your
supervisor that you have a rational, well thought out approach to
your work, that you know what you are about. It serves also the *
highly desirable function of protecting you from being accused *
later of having failed to achieve goals which you never intended *
to achieve anyway. *

Listed below are the information and details which should be covered in any proposal. We have omitted some of an administrative or operational nature—the amount of your time, support staff time, etc.—whose necessity you can judge better than we can. Any supervisor or manager will be justified in wanting to be informed on the matters listed. You will recognize also those items which are very clearly related to matters of Design. Perhaps less clearly related are matters such as where the group will meet and for how long, questions which may affect the types of activities you choose. In the skill training which will follow your study of this book, more details will be supplied.

1. Describe the characteristics of the members who will benefit from this group.

2. Indicate the purpose of the group, the barriers it proposes to overcome, program goals.

3. The principles around which sessions will be organized; of activities to be included; types of topics to be discussed.

4. How this type of group fits within CEIC guidelines and/or meets CEIC goals.

5. The degree to which these types of groups have been effective in the past.

6. Who will be leading the group and in what ways is he/she is prepared for this task.

7. The number of members who will be in the group; the selection (recruitment) procedures.

8. Where the group will meet; for how long; when will it begin and when will it end.

9. Evaluation procedures which are planned; if there will be a follow-up, if so what this will involve.

10. Types of problems you foresee and how you plan to handle them.

Once the detailed proposal has been prepared, it will need to be "sold" or at least "tried out": on supervisors, co-workers and potential members. You will require skill and sensitivity to ensure that the value of the group can be fully appreciated. Educating others about the potential value, as well as the realistic limitations of groups, as we have already indicated, is critical for success. You are looking for a sympathetic response to the kind of group being proposed. It is possible that you may have to modify or adapt the proposal in some way in order to gain the needed CEC support.

A Special Note

Throughout the period of negotiation, you must keep in mind the importance of obtaining sufficient space, materials and other resources in order to make the group operational. While general support and approval, acknowledgement that this group is a "good thing" and will help the CEC as well as the clients is necessary, it does not mean anything if you cannot have the needed services of clerical staff, access to equipment or budgetary support. Preparation requires careful thought.

Time for you, as the leaders, to make these preparations is usually overlooked. This time will not appear simply because you need it, you must plan for it as you plan everything else.

SELECTION OF GROUP MEMBERS

The first step in establishing a procedure for selection requires you to have a clear picture of what type of client will fit or not fit the parameters of the group. This perspective, to a large degree, emerges through the Needs Assessment and will have been specified very clearly in the Proposal.

The actual selection procedures often involve a number of * counsellors because they will individually assess and then refer * clients. Clearly, these colleagues ought to be familiar with the purpose of the group, and the types of members desired.

As we have seen, you will already have been wise enough to have obtained their opinions about the sort of group to be formed and/or in some way or another have taken colleagues into your confidence. Just the same, initial hesitations may have lingered or reappeared.

People may directly express their doubts. Conversely, you may sense an unspoken hesitancy. This is the time to ferret it out, for example: "I sense you are not very enthusiastic about this idea,"—any response that shows it is all right to express negative views and which indicates that you are prepared to listen.

If your proposal is challenged on practical grounds there is no substitute for having excellent reasons and justifications ready. It is important to remember, however, that hostility is often masked by a series of arguments which may seem completely "logical" or practical in nature and some persistence may be required to bring these negative feelings into the open where they can be discussed.

To ensure consistency in referrals from colleagues, you may, at this point, want to establish very clear guidelines for including suitable clients in the group. As an illustration, consider a situation where a career exploration group is being planned for youth. The guidelines for this group might be as follows:

(a) clients between the ages of 18 and 24;

(b) males and females;

(c) the member must be interested and willing to come to the group;

(d) the member must be grappling with career exploration issues; and

(e) the member must understand the purposes of the group.

It is worth the time, in this Planning Stage, to be certain that colleagues who might refer clients understand the guidelines and also that they understand the advantages of participation in the group. The last point: that they should be able to advocate group membership with some enthusiasm, has been much belaboured in this chapter, and we assume is now well understood by you. Let us assume that using skill and sensitivity you have achieved this important goal.

To establish what you mean by criteria, you might hold a meeting with referring counsellors, individually if necessary. You should certainly also distribute copies of the criteria for reference. Establishing the criteria for membership is essential. Haphazard referrals have the same result as a car backing up on the free way—one person going in the wrong direction and everyone else in a pile-up.

While you are clarifying with colleagues about who should be in a group, take the opportunity to clarify who should *not*:

- clients who appear to be extremely withdrawn and may need individual help or referral for personal or other counselling, (substance abusers, for example);

- clients who display persistent and extreme anger. They will dominate and impede the group from reaching its goals;

- clients with a lack of ability to speak or understand the working language of the group;

- most importantly, clients whose goals are not consistent with those of the group and this is sometimes an "iffy" proposition. Don't let colleagues use your group as a place to "unload" clients with whom they are making small progress (we speak from experience), on the grounds that these individuals will "do better" in a group. Lots of people do better in a group but not if they have needs which cannot be met in a group *or* if they have any of the characteristics just listed.

The ethical guidelines for group leaders developed by the Association for Specialists in Group Work (1980) highlights the importance of the selection procedure in the following statements (in Corey, 1985).

> The group leader shall conduct a pre-group interview with each prospective member for purposes of screening orientation and, in so far as possible, shall select group members whose needs and goals are compatible with the established goals of the group; who will not impede the group process; and whose well-being will not be jeopardized by the group experience (p. 66).

If it is possible for you to conduct a screening interview, you
should acquire enough information to decide whether a
particular client is a suitable candidate for the proposed group if
the client's goals match the proposed group goals. The techniques described in Module I for conducting an Assessment Interview would be helpful to review. In order to assess the degree
of matching, it is important to determine:

- the client's barriers to employment; and from this decide;

- the client's primary employability needs: support in building self-confidence? Job search strategies? A blend of both?
  Whatever they are, are they the same as the Program Goals?

- the client's experience of unemployment (i.e., length of
  time out of work, amount of experience in job search, reaction to not finding work, etc.) to ensure that she or he is not
  emotionally too far removed from where the other members will be;

- the client's attitude about working on his/her employment
  barriers in a group setting, or, to put this in Module 1 term,
  to achieve a "mutually agreed upon...action plan (the
  group) upon which the client is committed to work".

A key goal for you during the screening interview will be to orient prospective group members to the group's purpose, goals
and plans. Providing information about when the group starts,
where it will be held and the times is, of course, essential and reasonable, helps with decision and may relieve some normal anxiety. Letting clients know that other group members will have similar concerns will be reassuring.

Another (but not ideal and not recommended by us) scenario
for the formation of groups is one where potential group members come together without having direct access to a counsellor.
Perhaps there has been some advertising and people have signed
a sheet indicating their interest and intention to participate. Under these circumstances you must take particular care to ensure
that the advertising is accurate and sufficiently detailed to provide a clear idea of the purpose of the group.

In any case, it is always advisable to hold an information meet- *
ing for potential group members (in addition to any general in- *
formation sessions outlining all programs and services offered by *
CEIC). At this time, the group members would be told about the *
goals, procedures, activities and expected outcomes of the
group. Group members thus have the opportunity to meet the
leader (you) and one another. If they are uncertain about the
group they have the opportunity to do some preliminary checking before committing themselves. You also have the chance to
do some additional assessment and, possibly, some last minute
screening prior to the formal beginning of the group.

DEALING WITH DIFFICULTIES

What do you do when you are challenged by colleagues? Mana- *
gers and supervisors may be sympathetic to group counselling. *
Just the same, one experience shows that people without training *
may have expectations which are unrealistic and misunderstand- *
ings can occur. What resources and skills do you have that can be *
used? As you may have already gathered, the counselling and *
consultation skills described in the previous chapter for use with *
clients can be extremely useful in dealing with co-workers in the *
Planning Stage. Listed below are examples of problems and mis- *
understandings you may face, along with some strategies that can *
be used in meeting them. *

Questions from a supervisor and leader responses

a) A supervisor may accept the idea of group counselling, but
   not see how it can fit into the current schedule of activities
   because of a shortage of resources.

   Response: You need to listen carefully to your supervisor's
           hesitations. Keeping these concerns in mind, you
           might develop an outline which illustrates how time
           and resources can be better utilized by using the
           group approach. If the supervisor is still not
           convinced, you might suggest some short term

arrangement, such as a pilot project, with appropriate evaluation measures.

b) A supervisor may want to implement a group counselling program, but assign insufficient or inappropriate resources for the task.

Response: Rather than going forward with a group which is destined to fail, you should advise the supervisor of your doubts and concerns and suggest some alternatives, e.g., perhaps a reduced program which would be appropriate for the assigned resources.

Group counselling is a legitimate activity and group counsellors are professional people. It is probably clear that attempting to run a group without proper resources is impossible. To accept an allocation of inadequate resources is, in effect to promise what you cannot deliver.

Also, do explain why it is essential that you have adequate time to prepare for a group—and then stay within the agreed-upon number of hours!

c) You may feel that you have a great idea for a group, but be unable to obtain the necessary organizational approval for the group.

Response: You will have to withdraw and perhaps seek further clarification as to what would be acceptable and then re-think the idea. With additional consultation it might be possible to develop a proposal using some of the previous ideas in such a way as to offer something perceived by supervisors and colleagues as really needed.

d) A supervisor might agree with the idea of group counselling, assign you for the task and expect other counsellors to make the appropriate referrals.

Response: With the support of the supervisor you can go ahead with the project, but, as we know, the support of colleagues is not a sure thing. All the steps mentioned in this chapter: dealing with colleague ambivalence, setting up individual and/or group meetings, providing clear information about the nature and purpose of the program, issuing clear guidelines, are where you would next concentrate your energies.

e) You may find that some of the referrals are inappropriate, or that no one is being referred at all.

Response: When this happens you need to go back to the people making the referrals and clarify how they are making their decisions. Either people do not have the information right or you have not been able to deal with their worries and/or negative views of group counselling. This individual consultation is sometimes a key influence in getting clients referred to your group.

f) In a situation where membership in the group is determined by advertising, you may be dissatisfied with the type of people being attracted to the group.

Response: You should re-evaluate the message conveyed in the advertising. Ask clients coming to the groups and staff who are working in the front desks about the message that they have been getting—which, in this case, is obviously not the one you intended.

There are, of course, other problem situations which might arise. But with a crystal clear understanding of what groups can offer (plus the appropriate skills and training) you will be prepared to deal sensibly and adequately with difficulties as they arise.

HOW DESIGN AND PLANNING FIT TOGETHER

As we promised in the previous chapter, here is a schedule which indicates the way in which the Design component and the Planning Stage fit together. The schedule has been put together on the assumption that you will be doing all the planning from start to finish. It is best that you understand the entire process even if, in reading through, you mentally "edit-out" steps and decisions you know you will not take.

Planning	**The Design**

The Idea

(You, or possibly your manager)
A group for disadvantaged youth?
Mothers on welware?
People who want to make a
   career decision?

The Self-Check

Is this something that needs
   to be done?
Do I have the skill level?

The Needs Assessment

Review the literature.
Try out the idea on the manager,
   supervisors, colleagues.
Try out your ideas on clients
(The Group Employment Survey).
Make necessary adjustments,
   arrive at consensus.

> Note: While carrying out the Needs Assessment, check also to see what space may be needed and whether if it is available, and the same goes for any help which may be needed from support staff, supplies, equipment, etc.

The Proposal	Input for the Design
1. ...characteristics of the members...	What needs to be done? What are these clients unable to accomplish that the group will help them to accomplish? The deficits which characterize these clients.
2. The purpose of the group, the barriers...The Program Goals.	The Program Goals
3. The principles around which sessions will be organized ...types of activities... ...types of topics...	The learning principles, principles of group counselling which will apply and you will use. What the group will be doing (probably structured group activities). What you consider are the important aspects of the particular employment barriers the group will overcome.
4. How this type of group fits within CEIC guidelines and/or meets CEIC goals.	
5. The degree to which these types of groups have been effective/successful in the past.	
6. Who will be leading...	
7. ...number of members ...selection (recruitment) procedures	

8. Where the group will meet
...how long

9. Evaluation procedures...   What can be done relevant to
   follow-up   Program Goals?

10. Types of problems...   Flexibility/adaptability
    you foresee   required

**Submission of the proposal for
Organizational Approval**

Make any Adjustments   Adjust "Input for the Design"
Necessary   above.

Developing the Design

- Determine the program goals
  (already done)

- Translate the program goals
  into employment barriers to
  be overcome (already done)

- Operationalize the goals:
  Identify the specific
  knowledge, behaviour,
  experiential deficiencies
  which constitute the barriers;
  Specify the behavioural
  outcomes the clients will be
  able to demonstrate as a
  result of participating in the
  group which will indicate that
  these deficiencies have been
  corrected.

- Examine goals in relation to
  time available; make
  adjustments as necessary.

- Examine goals in relation to setting and circumstances: space available and whether support staff will be available, if their help is necessary.

- Develop (and/or select) and sequence structured activities (strategies) or carefully examine a prepared Program Package keeping in mind:

Purpose-goal-activity-outcome relationship;
Observation-rehearsal-feedback needs;
Cognitive-behavioural-affective components.
Stages of group development starting with the easiest and building.
De-briefing activities.

- The need to build in some adaptability: develop or select alternate activities.

Check the design: Run down the list of all the outcomes—if they were achieved, would the client have overcome employment barriers?

Select Group Members

- referrals from colleagues, dealing with colleagues' ideas and attitudes,

establishing and distributing
the guidelines

• screen potential members,   **Checking the design**—a
orient them to group's   user's check
purpose and goals

Implement   **Implement**

                                Evaluation (at Termination and
                                Post-Group Stages

POINTS TO REMEMBER

  • **Careful work at the Planning Stage is an essential and
    fundamental element in determining the success or failure
    of the employment group.**

  • **Several activities are important in the Planning Stage:**

    - **conducting a Needs Assessment**
    - **developing a proposal**
    - **promoting the proposed group with colleagues and
      supervisors**
    - **applying counselling skills in dealing with questions and
      possible reluctance from co-workers**
    - **carefully selecting potential group members**
    - **orienting potential members to the up-coming group.**

POINTS TO PONDER

1. Think about the types of employment groups you might like
   to run in the CEC where you work.

2. Think about sources of support and opposition to running a
   group in your CEC setting. What strategies could you use to
   overcome any barriers that you foresee?

EXERCISES

1. Write a short outline of a proposal for the employment group of your choice. **Bring this proposal to the training program.**

2. To whom, in your office, would you show your detailed pro-posal?

3. If you are forming a homogeneous group, what do you see as the advantages?

4. If you are not, what do you see as holding the group together? How do you see these differing members as able to help each another?

Chapter 7

Initial Stage

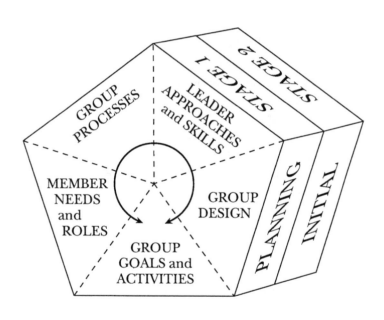

OVERVIEW

"Well begun is half done." Group employment counselling is no exception to this rule. The leader always hopes to get off to a good start because a good beginning goes a long way to ensuring a "good" middle and a "good" end.

By the end of the Planning Stage, you will have secured permission to run your group, completed operational arrangements and have developed an appropriate design. You also know your members.

At this stage you will concentrate your efforts in the following areas:

- initiating and maintaining group interaction,
- helping members to feel included,
- developing and supporting group cohesion,
- modelling the behaviours (around processes) which you want group members to adopt,
- assisting members to explore their individual goals within the context of program goals.

At the completion of this stage you will have brought group members to the point where they feel included within the group and can identify with its expressed goals. Members will be approaching the point where they will be able to consider a need to change.

OBJECTIVES

As a result of reading this chapter, you will be competent to:

1. **describe the characteristics of the Initial Stage,**

2. **describe how the program goals articulated in the Planning Stage serve to focus the group initially,**

3. **describe member needs common at this stage and identify the subsequent roles evolving from these needs,**

4. **explain the importance of group processes in the Initial Stage,**

5. **outline and provide the rationale for the leader approaches and skills needed to guide group members in the Initial Stage,**

6. **specify effective leadership interventions in response to specific member roles or individual behaviour, and**

7. **describe the most important principles which you should follow in selecting and developing activities.**

CHARACTERISTICS OF THE INITIAL STAGE

Dominating everything which happens at this early stage is the preoccupation of members with uncertainties about acceptance. Acceptance is not simply: Will they like and accept me? Although as members of the human race, we all know how important that question is. But in this case, acceptance is also: Do I accept them? Are their goals my goals? Are we all going to the same place? Am I going to be odd-one-out?

Other important matters, for example, norms about the behaviour of members and the leader are discussed and, in some degree, settled at this stage. Expectations about the values of the group, worries and uncertainties about being in it, are expressed. Not unexpectedly, members are still not entirely certain (despite your care in the pre-group interview) if they want to be involved and how, and they may look to you to give direction. All of these steps reflect member absorption with their need for acceptance and their uncertainty about whether they fit in.

Questions which members frequently ask sometimes, (as we learn later) only of themselves, in the Initial Stage are listed below:

• How is this type of group going to help me get a job?

The uncertainty is:

Do I have the same goals as these people?

Am I going to have to do a lot of stuff that will be pointless?

- How can I talk about what I really think or feel in front of a group of strangers?

The uncertainty is:

Is this going to be embarrassing?

- What is going to happen here? What will this experience be like?

The uncertainty is:

Is this my bag? Are they going to make me do things I hate? Lay a trip on me?

- Who are the other people here? What are they like?

The uncertainty is:

Am I in there with a lot of people I don't approve of, a bunch of losers? Will they disapprove of me?

- Where do I fit in with these people? How will I be treated here?

The uncertainty is:

Will they understand me? Are they going to do a lot of that: "Honestly, it's-for-your-own-good!" nonsense?

These questions are indications of the concerns of group members. Taken together they account for major characteristics of this Initial Stage. Corey (1983. p.191) described some of these characteristics, which we have re-grouped into the following sub-headings:

Concerns, Behaviours, and **Learning**.

Concerns

- Members are deciding whom they can trust, how much they   *
will disclose, how safe the group is, whom they like and dislike,   *
and how much to get involved. (You can see the acceptance   *
theme: Can I trust them to accept me? Or should I play it
cool? Will they still like me if I tell them about the time...?)

Behaviours

- Participants test the atmosphere and get acquainted. *

- They generally display socially acceptable behaviour: in other *
  words, risk-taking is relatively low and exploration is tentative. *

- Some negative feelings may initially surface, a form of testing to *
  determine if all feelings are acceptable. *

- Periods of silence and awkwardness arise; members may look *
  for direction from the leader. (You can see the tentative *
  character of the involvement, "get acquainted" as opposed to
  "making friends", "periods of silence" when someone else may
  take the risk.)

Learning

- Members begin to learn the norms and what is expected: learn *
  how the group functions; and learn how to participate in a *
  group. *

- Members are learning the basic attitudes of respect, empathy, *
  acceptance, caring, and responding—all attitudes that facilitate *
  trust-building. These attitudes are a sub-set of all the norms *
  which members are beginning to learn; some of them will be
  made explicit and some will be implicit. All will be modelled by
  the leader. (This learning is just the beginning; it shares the tentative, toe-in-the-water quality of the Concerns and Behaviour.)

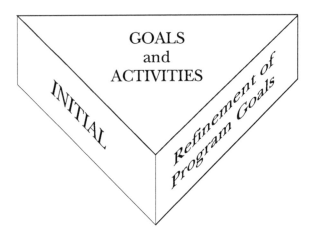

GROUP GOALS AND ACTIVITIES

Two important goals need to be understood by members in the Initial Stage: *Program Goals* and *Group Goals.*

Program goals constitute the purpose for convening the group. Within an employment counselling context, the program goals are explicit, whatever their focus may be, such as: career exploration, job search, self-confidence building, with supporting behavioural goals which are very clearly detailed. While these goals remain, in a general sense, constant throughout the life of the group some adjustments will be necessary in every case because—as we stated at the beginning of this book—every group is somewhat different. In the Initial Stage you will be called upon   *
to make the Program Goals explicit to ensure that the goals are   *
met so far as possible. This action reflects the commitment you   *
made to your organization during the Planning Stage.   *
　　Members will feel some commitment to the Program Goals   *
but will endeavour to personalize them so that they fit more ac-   *
curately to their individual needs. It is very important that this   *
link, between Program Goals and individual needs, be estab-   *
lished. The results will be the Group Goals.   *

Group Goals are arrived at through an exploration of members' *
perceptions as to the way the Program Goals will, or will not, *
assist them to achieve their individual goals. This discussion is *
followed by a process which seeks to find the commonalities
among these individual goals: these commonalities become the
goals for the group: The Grop Goals. Here is an indication of the
way Program Goals become Group Goals.

You will have done a pre-group interview with members; they
have, therefore, been told what the Program Goals are. But it
happens to all of us that when we come to an anticipated activity,
especially a new one, as this group will be, that matters are not
exactly as we had thought they would be.

To begin with, human communications are not always
perfect. In the pre-group interview perhaps you have not been
perfectly clear or perhaps the potential member, like so many of
us, fails to think of very important questions until the interview is
over. It can happen that when you describe a goal, the listener
understands something a little different. It may also happen that
members "fix things up" in their minds so that "of course" this or
the other matter will be dealt with, or "for sure" they won't be
doing (x) or (y) and "of course" it will be unreasonable to expect
me to do (a) or (b). Anticipation, in brief, is rarely the same as
the reality.

Let us suppose that, when the group meets, you have described the program goals. You do a consensus to check that
members subscribe to these goals. Katinka may say that she knew
that the goals were (say) job search but never realized they would
include evaluation of career options. She is certain she knows
what she wants to do and believes this activity will be a waste of
time. You will invite her to say more. She may give a good reason
or describe a fear. You might also check the reactions of other
members: Do they agree? Do they have the same worries?

You do have a duty to explain that this element has been included because experience has shown it to be necessary. (Maybe
add that people sometimes get "locked in" by a premature
choice.) It is to be hoped that Katinka will see your point. In any
case, you need to assure her that her concerns will be respected.
She will not be forced to be involved. You may suggest that she

wait and see what she feels like when the matter comes up. If she is willing, she could help others who are concerned with evaluation of options (she may learn something too). If the whole group is uncertain, you provide the same kind of assurance and offer some kind of compromise. In the case of Katinka, if you are able to be empathic and responsive, she will very probably feel that her needs can be fitted in within the program goals.

It may be that Fred now wants to add a goal. You support the idea, certainiy a good one, but say you are not certain the time will stretch. Again you may check with other members: do they also think this goal should be included? If they really want it in, you may work with them to see how it might be included. If it is a small matter, it might be substituted for another small matter. If it cannot in any way be accommodated, you are not obliged to jettison another essential goal. But you may help members find a way, outside of the group, to achieve what they want.

This may be one of the first occasions on which you model communication, norms of respect and acceptance and ways of decision making which you hope group members will adopt. This demonstration of respect and acceptance can result in individual group members experiencing an increased sense of motivation and commitment to group goals.

This process of identifying Group Goals will also involve group members in setting criteria needed to assess the achievement of the goals which they have been agreed upon, and will help them to understand expected rewards or outcomes of goals achievement. Finally, and perhaps most importantly, your leadership in the Initial Stage will assist group members to perceive and understand that they are participating in a group that provides a structure for learning but allows for an individual sense of control over involvement and goal attainment.

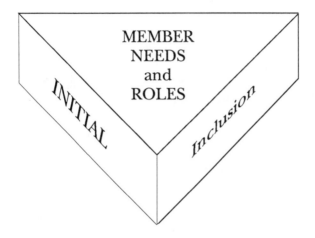

MEMBER NEEDS AND ROLES

Do I belong here?

Uneasiness concerning inclusion or belonging dominates members at this time. People worry about whether the group will understand and include them, not because they are worried about this particular group, but because they habitually worry about whether they will be understood and included. They may experience a fairly high level of tension precisely because they fear rejection. Certainly people cannot attend to work at hand or work on stated objectives until they feel accepted. Schultz (1973) emphasizes that a sense of inclusion forms the basis for (i.e., precedes) trust formation—vital and necessary for a productive group.

This overwhelming and dominating need for inclusion un- *
derlies and motivates the roles which members often assume in *
the Initial Stage of a group. Many of the common roles are listed *
below. We have described them as they manifest themselves in relation to a number of different thrusts or purposes (and sometimes in relation to cross-purposes) of group activities. Generally these roles are:

a) roles which function to promote the accomplishment of *task*   *
   and the realizing of group goals. (Helping each other   *
   complete activities, etc.).   *

b) roles which function to create a supportive climate in the   *
   group or building of *maintenance*. (Supporting ideas of other
   members or the other members, themselves, acknowledging
   feelings of other members, etc.)

c) roles, some quite definitely individual (i.e., not frequently   *
   shared by others), which do not contribute to task or   *
   maintenance and are seen as *hindering* roles, (Changing the   *
   subject, putting other members down, etc.)

Remember that socially acceptable behaviour predominates at this stage so you are more likely to see the roles which contribute to task or maintenance.

In the interest of keeping the entire picture in mind, it is also important to remember that the "good" roles do not necessarily spring from a less worried individual. People tend to deal with tension differently. When things go wrong, some rely on very conforming behaviours, other more obviously, raise Cain. You cannot assume less discomfort in either one, you can assume the same need to be protected in a group setting.

You cannot completely stop hindering roles. Disparaging (or despairing) remarks should be dealt with by the good use of leader skills, empathy, paraphrasing, and supporting. (Their use will be described in greater detail later in this chapter).

Roles Related to Task Actions

Information and Opinion Seeker. In this role the member asks for facts, data and information relevant to the group's goals and activities. He/she asks for opinions, feelings and/or reactions to issues raised and ideas presented.

Roles Related to Maintenance Actions

Tension Reliever. The individuals in this role offer what students of Shakespeare call "comic relief". They inject humour in a timely and appropriate fashion to help members relax when tension or frustration has become so great that the group is no longer productive. A Tension Reliever may suggest a break from the group's activities for the same purpose. These people are also, naturally, helping themselves.

Harmonizer. This member attempts to reconcile or mediate different positions, opinions and points of view held by other members. This person also demonstrates a willingness to back off somewhat from his or her own point of view when it is in conflict with the views of others. Harmonizers have sometimes become what they are as a result of bad experiences with conflict. Their efforts are usually welcome, but Harmonizers can be a problem if they persist in simply trying to "cement over" differences which must be settled.

Encourager. This member is supportive, friendly and responsive to others; demonstrating interest and respect for other people, their ideas and their values; shows awareness of, and concern for others. Usually the Encourager has received reinforcement for encouraging, may also be reassuring him or herself, or seeking reciprocal encouragement. Whatever the reason, it is hard to object to having an Encourager in the group.

Roles Related to Hindering Actions

Dominater. This member tries to take over personal control * through the use of power, authority, and direct control or by ma- * nipulative means such as flattery. Frequently, they simply take up * more "air time." This person may simply have got into a great * many bad interpersonal habits, but people who try to control are * usually uncomfortable about what may happen if things get *out* of control. The Dominater often makes people angry without their being quite certain why, in other words this is not an overtly offensive person.

Recognition Seeker. This member tries to impress others with her/ * his importance, success, experience or knowledge, attempting *

to gain status by impressing others rather than by using knowl-   *
edge and experience to help the group move ahead. This person
may be uncertain about his or her competence to accomplish
goals but still long for inclusion.

Aggressor. This member criticizes other members and their ideas   *
in a hostile fashion; tries to "put down" or aggressively defeat   *
others; may try to belittle others directly or by means of hostile   *
humour. The Aggressor is a very familiar type who puts him or
herself "up" by putting other people "down". The Aggressor, in
other words, is often openly disagreeable or offensive.

Special Interest Pleader. This member attempts to turn the group
into an audience to talk to about some irrelevant special interest
such as political beliefs, "big government," or "what's wrong with
the world today." He/she carries in his/her mind a permanent
"letter from home" which states why he/she need not put out an
effort: "My needs are special!"

Withdrawer. This member demonstrates no concern, interest or
participation in what the group is engaged in; has the body but
not the mind present; sometimes takes even the "body" from the
group by leaving because of lack of interest. This individual may
have learned that it is "safer" to go unnoticed. Like every other
member, she or he probably has a lot to offer and will repay the
patience and effort necessary to elicit her/his input.

Grandstander. This member unproductively uses the group's time
with unrelated humour, practical jokes and/or "show-boat" cynical remarks. Like the Dominator, this person may be displaying
habitual behaviour, always "fools around" (maybe a reason to be
fired), probably afraid to get serious and/or really try.

The roles related to task and maintenance actions obviously
need to be encouraged, while those which are hindering need to
be minimized. The positive atmosphere which will result, allows
members to feel included and is conducive to greater group
cohesion, the most important goal for this stage.

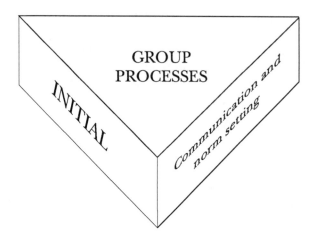

GROUP PROCESSES

Everything that happens in a group takes place within the context of the flow of interaction and to speak of interaction is to refer to group processes.

Two major group processes are crucial in the Initial Stage—communication and norm development. Both of these processes are fundamental to the achievement of group cohesion. You, as leader, must set the tone for communication between yourself and group members and also among group members. In addition, you will help the group to establish norms.

Communication

The communication process is given a good start in this, the Initial Stage. It is hardly necessary to emphasize the role which good communication plays in developing group cohesion because it builds and facilitates effective understanding. Obviously, with good communication, people are better able to make known their goals and wishes, identify ways in which they are like each other and have common interests, and perceive either other's reactions and intentions accurately .

In short, good communication confers in this situation the * same benefits as it does in all others: the capacity for intellectual * and emotional understanding. Life for human beings is infinitely * more difficult when communications are poor. In the short, time-tight and limited group counselling situation, you have an important role to play by ensuring that the communication process is the best it can be.

You will receive important assistance in doing so from the fact that you will be working with structured learning activities. Research has demonstrated that, in a group which is structured, where the emphasis is on learning—the sort under discussion in this book—information is communicated more effectively, openly, honestly and accurately than it is in groups which tend to be unstructured and competitive in nature. The reason is that the structured learning activity precludes material of a threatening and highly personal nature from arising. The structure, then, provides a degree of safety because the group is going to look at carefully selected and circumscribed behaviour only and these behaviours are related to quite specific goals. People have very little (if any) need to be indirect, devious or hesitant in expressing themselves. They are not called upon to justify—as they might be in a less structured group for example—a long history of neurotic behaviour or why they never have any friends. The result is that defensive communication is much less likely to occur. Self-disclosure about non-threatening matters may be high, increasing the information available to members for learning and mobilizing resources. This learning structure therefore provides a reasonably safe arena within which communication may occur. And you are certainly not called upon to clarify the unconscious meanings which in another group might be attached to client communication.

The communication skills which you would like members to start learning are active listening, clarifying, paraphrasing, sum- * marizing and linking. All of these are also counselling skills * which you have learned as the result of training, you will therefore not expect a high-level performance from members at the start. You can teach these skills; in part, by reinforcing them whenever they appear.

You may also teach skills by making them part of structured learning activities. In an activity which involves interviewing, members may be urged to use active listening with some clarifying and paraphrasing. When small groups join to compare conclusions you may do some linking: "It seems that everyone agrees that...", then you may ask the group to link: "Can anyone find anything else all the groups had in common?" You might follow the same procedure with summarizing. At the start you provide a summary; later, you may ask a group member to summarize.

Your role as a model is also very important in teaching communication skills. The fact that you model empathy, support, etc., will have a real influence on the group. It is not unlikely that you will hear your own expressions being used by group members. You also model non-verbal communication. If your patterns of communication are habitually argumentative or critical, the group's will be the same. It is your persistent verbal and non-verbal communication, of empathy, warmth and openness which, absorbed by members, will help to make the group safe and secure and open it up to free, relaxed communication. If you model empathy and respect, so will the group.

Norms

All groups possess a basic set of rules or guidelines to promote the constructive interactions which allow members to get on with the group's work. Norms represent the perceptions, beliefs and values of individual members (coached perhaps by you) regarding how they and all the members should behave and interact.

Norms can be explicit or implicit. Explicit norms are easily recognized by members and may exist in written form like the notices next to the copying machine. They can be established effectively during the first group session through group discussion and common agreement. Norms which you will probably want to establish explicitly would deal with confidentiality, rules for feed-back and perhaps some sort of rule about no put down remarks. More clear-cut norms might be to do with punctuality or rules about smoking.

Implicit norms refer to the "unwritten rules" that guide the group. These norms can exert a powerful influence and are, in large measure, "implicit" in your behaviour as leader and, therefore, determined by you. An important example is that people do not disclose beyond their level of comfort in the group. Another might be that members do not interrupt each other. Another norm will develop implicitly from the way in which you deal with members who may be hostile, angry or in any way displaying less than optimal behaviour. Your use of empathy and support sends a clear message that, in this group, everyone is entitled to understanding, respect and dignity. When you use consensus taking or moderating, you model the norm that everyone's views are important. It may also be that a norm develops with the result that whoever sits nearest the radiator decides when to open or close the window or that there is a norm that remarks about (say) the local transport company are always considered funny.

Johnson & Johnson (1982, p. 398) have suggested a set of general guidelines to assist leaders in establishing and maintaining norms in the Initial Stage of group development. They emphasize the principle that, if members are to accept norms, they must recognize that they exist, that other people accept them and they must feel some sense of internal commitment. The commitment comes from understanding how the norms will support goal accomplishment and you may, sometimes, clarify this relationship. Members will accept and internalize norms for which they feel a sense of ownership. Members may need examples (in addition to your modelling); they may even need the chance to practise.

Because norms exist to help group effectiveness, they should be flexible, so that, at any time, more appropriate norms can be substituted. Norms established around principles of individual dignity and worth, naturally, do not change.

In the Initial Stage, several norms will be established. At this stage, whatever is done should serve the goal of cohesion. Norms should be established regarding:

• responsibilities of group members—probably, through discussion; *
*

• behaviours expected of members - matters such as schedules, * coffee breaks, etc., can be established through (relatively) * straight-forward discussion. Others, such as how to give feed- * back, may require careful use of leader skills. These more diffi- * cult subjects, may not arise at this stage; *

• procedures for making decisions within the group—again * through discussion, but very likely also with some early model- * ling by you—the consensus-taking, moderating skills, for exam- * ple, referred to earlier; *

• methods for handling differences of opinion in the group— * modelled by you, using linking; *

• the style of communication between yourself and members— * and among group members—(discussed previously) is of * course intensely modelled by you. Communication may also be * strongly influenced—for good or ill— by one or more of the * "internal" leaders. In this case you will use leader skills: * support, immediacy, gentle confronting to achieve the norms * which are desirable. *

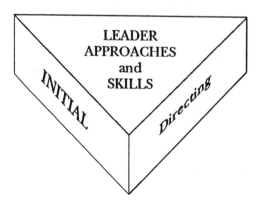

LEADER APPROACHES AND SKILLS

The needs of members in this stage inevitably determine the *
approaches and skills that you will be required to use in *
interacting with group members. What follows is a series of *
member statements that reflect member roles, already described
in more general terms earlier in this chapter, which are typical of
the Initial Stage. Here, we will demonstrate the work you will do
in response to the members' needs and roles. For example, the
member's statement is provided along with the identified role
and possible member feelings. Next, a leader's response is
provided and categorized according to approach and skills. Note *
that the leader responds to both the feelings and content that is *
being expressed. In doing so, the leader is also modelling com- *
munication patterns and, therefore, establishing norms. Fre- *
quently, your leader statements will also promote feelings of in- *
clusion by group members that will help make the group *
cohesive. *

Member Statements and Leader Responses

1. *Statement:*

   "I would like to get clear what we should be discussing in
   our groups. I know that each of us will be sharing our frus-
   trations. Now, how should I be responding to what is being
   said—should I take notes or just listen?"

Role:	Information and Opinion Seeker.
Feeling:	Uncertain, confused about procedures.
	May be very concerned to "do well"
Unspoken:	"Am I OK?"

   Response:

   "That's a good question. It's really important to get the instructions clear in your mind before doing the activity.
   Here is one suggestion that seems to work for many group
   members."

Approach: Directing.
Skills: Clarifying, information giving, modelling,
          understanding, reinforcing
Unspoken: "You're OK!"

2. *Statement:*

"I really don't need any more rides on an emotional, roller
coaster. Out at the Ex, they call it the Big Dipper and it
always makes me sick."

Role: Tension reliever (Maintenance Action).
Feeling: Tense—wanting relief.
Unspoken: "I want to get away from here! (from this
pain!)"

Response:

"Laughing...I guess most people feel the way you do—even
one ride is too many. I like your idea of getting away from
emotional ups and downs, let's brainstorm some ways of
doing that."

Approach: Directing.
Skill: Empathy, supporting, reinforcing.
Unspoken: "You're right! Let's get away from here!
          (Dump that pain by making some changes!)"

3. *Statement:*

"I think that you both are really addressing some of my
concerns. I am interested in working hard at job search,
but I can also see the value of taking care of myself. In a
way, you're just talking about different sides of the same
coin."

Role: Harmonizer (Maintenance action).
Feeling: Tension and discomfort with group
          interaction.
Unspoken: "If I don't step in, something bad will happen!"

Response:

"John, you've hit the nail on the head! It really isn't an either–or issue, both Ted and Mary have addressed important parts of the issue and they really are different sides of the same coin. Let's look at the whole coin more closely."

Approach: Directing.
Skills: Supporting, clarifying, linking and summarizing.
Unspoken: "That was a good move you made! Don't worry, I'll help to work for harmony, too."

4. *Statement:*

"I'm really pleased that you're in this group. You've had so many different experiences and I know that I am going to learn a lot through our discussion."

Role: Encourager (Maintenance Action).
Feeling: Satisfaction and hopefulness.
Unspoken: "I'm glad you're here."

Response:

"That's right, Sue! It's good to recognize the valuable input that other members can make! What they say can help you to figure other ways to be more successful in your own job search. Let's brainstorm some other ways that members' input may help the group."

Approach: Directing.
Skills: Supporting, clarifying, paraphrasing.
Unspoken: "You're a helpful person."

5. *Statement:*

"I guess I am supposed to talk about what we discussed, but to tell you the truth we got off track and started swapping airline stories. We managed to rank order the top three stories this year. Maybe I should share with you what's at the top of the list."

Role: Grandstanding (Hindering Action).
Feeling: Fear of rejection and increasing anxiety.
Unspoken: "Please don't make me deal with this! I can't handle this!"

Response:

"Fred, it seems to me that every time we start to talk about, 'what if I don't get a job after the first interview,' you begin to joke. I am wondering if your jokes cover up a fear of being rejected and that makes you very anxious. My hunch is that you aren't the only person in this group who worries about rejection. We all worry about it! Could we look at what happens when you try to deal with this sort of thing?"

Approach: Directing/Influencing.
Skills: Limiting, confronting, empathy, support, immediacy.
Unspoken: "I know you're scared! It's OK to be scared. It's not OK to hide from the problem. We all can confront the fear of rejection together!"

6. *Statement:*

"I have a better idea than discussing this in small groups. You are the leader and I would really like to hear what you have to say. When the group tries to solve it, it's often just a pooling of ignorance." (Sharp voice)

Role: Dominator (Hindering Action).
Feeling: Desperation and then irritation.
Unspoken: "Let's get on with it! These losers don't know anything. Just tell me what to do."

Response:

"You are really worried about how productive a group discussion would be on this issue. It might seem efficient to get my ideas and answers on the topic. I guess that I have found in the time I have spent running groups that my answers generally fit for some people and don't fit at all for others. I am sure that discussing it together will give you a broader range of good ideas that you may find helpful. I'd like to ask you to give it a try."

Approach:	Directing.
Skills:	Empathy, moderating, modelling.
Unspoken:	"I know you are worried you won't get what you want, things cannot be exactly as you would like. You and the group do have a lot of information between you. We can't let you call all the shots just because you are worried."

7. *Statement:*

"From what I've heard up to now, you all don't really know what's happening out there. Preparing a resumé isn't going to get you any closer to getting a job—there aren't any jobs, that's the problem. I don't intend to spend any time spinning my wheels writing resumés." (Angry tone)

Role:	Aggressing (Hindering Action).
Feeling:	Fears, anxiety.
Unspoken:	"I'm scared! I'm worried! I'm hopeless! I can't mobilize myself to do this task!"

Response:

"It sounds like you're feeling really discouraged and defeated about ever finding a job. And you're wondering if it's really worth your effort to do a resumé. Sometimes doing a resumé can seem like a big discouraging pain in the neck. It does seem to be an absolute necessity, though. I'd like you to give it a try. I will help in any way I can. "

Approach:	Directing.
Skills:	Empathy and paraphrasing, information-giving.
Unspoken:	"I really understand how worried you feel! And I know you feel really discouraged. But I will help you. "

8. *Statement:*

"Finding a career is easy if you're rich and have money behind you. When you're on welfare and have a couple of kids it's another story. Do you know what I make on welfare?" (Helpless posture and high squeaky voice.)

Role:	Special interest pleading (Hindering Action).
Feeling:	Fear, despair, outrage. Feeling like a victim.
Unspoken:	"Things are worse for me because I'm on welfare (a woman, an ex-offender, etc.). I can't be expected to deal with the world like other people!"

Response:

"You sound pretty scared and desperate about your chances of finding a career—especially as being on welfare has really limited your money and maybe your opportunities. My hunch is that many of you may be in a similar situation —that there are special barriers keeping you from finding work. It makes you feel angry because everything seems so difficult. I'd like to hear from some of the rest of you about this. Maybe later we can brainstorm as a group about ways to get around these barriers."

Approach:	Directing.
Skills:	Empathy, linking, restatement.
Unspoken:	"I am listening! I know you are angry and

worried. But let's look at ways you might get around your difficulties."

9. *Statement:*

"I've been to over 50 interviews and think that I've a few things to say about that topic. I've probably got more interviews under my belt than everyone in this room."

Role:	Recognition seeking (Hindering Action).
Feeling:	Isolated, not included.
Unspoken:	"Pay attention to me! I am an extraordinary, unusual person with special knowledge of this subject!"

Response:

"Jan, your experiences will be most valuable to the group! I sense a real frustration with the job interview techniques you've learned! And some hopelessness, too, since you haven't found a job. Maybe you could tell the group about what has happened to you in interviews."

Approach:	Directing.
Skills:	Supporting, empathy, paraphrase, information giving.
Unspoken:	"I do notice you! You are special! I've noticed you're sad, too! Here's how you can relate to the group."

10. *Behaviour:*

(Sheila is observed to be turned away somewhat from the group and has not spoken during the session.)

Role:	Withdrawing (Hindering Action)
Feeling:	Isolation, anxiety, fear of rejection or "put-downs", (possibly) anger.
Unspoken:	"If I say anything, they'll think I'm stupid. They don't like me so I'm not going to talk!"

Response:

"Sheila, I notice you sitting very quietly and I think we need your in-put. What do you think about all this?"

Approach: Directing/Influencing.
Skills: Immediacy, supporting, questioning.
Unspoken: "I see you sitting there not talking. It's OK! It's safe! We want to know what you think. You count!"

The illustrations that have been provided describe specific responses to a variety of member role statements (behaviours). These responses utilize leader skills and approaches and help to further the development of group progress. In addition to these illustrations, a list of practical leader suggestions may be useful to leaders in helping group members.

Practical Suggestions for the Leader in the Initial Stage

Setting Up

• Arrange seating so that members can hear and see one another.

• Consider carefully the size of sub-grouping, people still feel shy at this stage; the greater the uneasiness, the smaller the group.

• Randomly assign individuals to small groups. This method promotes interaction, inclusion.

• Structure learning experiences with goals that the individual member cannot meet by working alone.

Communicating

Follow the principles of good listening:

• focus on the speaker, look at the speaker and signal you are listening,

• don't be afraid of silence,

• restate or summarize what you've heard,

• respond to the feeling in messages,

• make linking statements in discussion.

The workshop will provide an opportunity to practice some of these states.

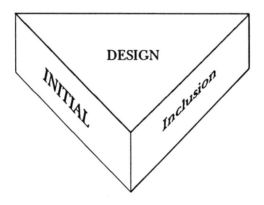

DESIGN

The key structured activities which you will select or develop for use in the Initial Stage will encourage members to become oriented to each other and the way things will be done in the group. The content of the activities must be recognizable as rele- *
vant to the reasons they are in the group (Group Goals) and the *
procedure be active and reassuring. In other words, the activity *
should seem reasonable and be something which members can *
do comfortably. *
    In designing or selecting activities for this stage you should have in mind that when members leave the group they should feel that they are doing well, that they have performed adequately or as well as anyone else (that they are "with" the group, a form of inclusion) and probably that the group is a good idea (a first form of cohesion) and that they have made a comforting and good start on achieving their employment goals.
    At this stage you will want to select an outcome which has an *
immediate appeal, a very apparent relationship to the group *

goals. At the same time, keep it simple and attainable. Do not, *
for example, choose an outcome which you know has a lot of
uncertainty and tension around it: choosing a career, if I find a
job who will look after my children? or any subject which you
know from experience makes clients tense.

You need a procedure, what they are going to do, that is reas- *
suring and simple. Talking in dyads is a clear example; most peo- *
ple can manage this much. Most people cannot get up and perform a skill before the entire group at the first meeting.

You do need interaction and talking in dyads is the least possi- *
ble interaction. It is also a first step toward inclusion. You can in- *
crease the interaction by having the dyads split up until every
one has been a dyad with everyone else. Now you have a little
more inclusion.

You may work on some easy, early communication skills by
asking one partner to paraphrase what the other has said (you
don't use the technical term): Is this what you said? I think you
told me...Then the first person may clarify: Well not exactly... or
what I meant was...Members will gradually get the idea. You will
bring everyone together to report what has happened. You link
and summarize to promote cohesion.

Above, we have described a classic inclusion or "icebreaker"
exercise, laid out in its separate parts. What you may do is
increase the difficulty in any part, that is: increase the size of the
discussion groups, require a more complicated answer or activity *
(rank order, describe what worries you, see if you can figure *
out), always trying to ensure that members will have a sense of *
achievement, that they have got to know each other a little better *
and that everyone has taken an additional step toward goal *
achievement. *

Important principles which underlie the implementation of
any group activity are:

- describe explicit outcomes for activities;

- always explain what will happen in the group, in other
  words, what is coming up in general and what is coming up
  next;

- structure learning experiences with goals that the individual
  member cannot meet by working alone.

Later, when the group is in the Working Stage, you will ask for more challenging activities involving greater risk taking.

Example of a Structured Design Activity

The following is an example of a specific activity that is appropriate at this stage. It has been designed to bring about a sense of member inclusion.

TITLE: INTRODUCTION ACTIVITY

Time Required: 50 minutes

Goals

1. to enable group members to learn one another's name.
2. to provide for initial interpersonal contact.
3. to permit members to learn additional information about the other participants' purposes for attending this group program.

Group size

large group and dyads

Materials

name tags, flip chart, felt pen

Physical Setting

large open space with chairs

Description of Activity:

Provide for meeting needs of inclusion among members of a new group.

Procedure:

1. Members secure name tags and seat themselves (2 min.)
2. Leader introduces self and states own interest in running group (3 min.).
3. Leader introduces the activity (15 min.):
   - announces the purpose,
   - assigns participants to dyads by instructing each to select the person on his or her immediate left (if extra person, leader joins dyad),
   - asks members to select role as Speaker and Listener,
   - indicates to the Listener that he/she is to ask the speaker the following questions (may write them on a flip chart): "What name do you wish to be called by in the group?" "Where are you from, and what non-work interest(s) do you have or, is there something about your family you'd like to describe?" "What is your purpose for attending this program?"
4. Once the speaker has answered these questions, (about 3 minutes) the dyad switches roles and repeats the above exchange.
   - the task is to listen carefully to the speaker as you will be asked to introduce your partner to the large group.
5. At the end of this exchange, members are told to check with each other if anything has been mentioned which they would not like brought back to the large group during the introduction of partners.
6. Members are told to make notes, if they wish, during the one-to-one exchange.
7. Group is asked to re-form into a large group.

8. The leader instructs members to begin their introductions (if extra member, leader begins the introductions [modelling]). If not, the leader asks for a volunteer to begin the introduction (15 min.).

9. After introductions are complete, the leader makes a summary statement about the members of the group (15 min.).

> e.g., "Our group sounds motivated and interested; and appears to have a common sense of purpose."

POINTS TO REMEMBER

- **A central concern for members at this stage is inclusion (Do I belong?). When inclusion is realized, trust is established and creates a working climate which facilitates goal attainment.**

- **In this stage the leader and the members are challenged to integrate program goals and individual expectations. This integration results in group goals which define the purpose for the group.**

- **Group processes that facilitate group dynamics in the Initial Stage are communication and the establishment of norms.**

- **The leader's approach largely involves directing members, using active listening, empathy, linking, information-giving, clarifying, paraphrasing, summarizing, supporting, immediacy and gently confronting.**

POINTS TO PONDER

In the group that you may be planning for your CEC office there will probably be a need to establish some norms.

What do you think these might be?

Which, if any, do you think might present the most difficulty?

How might you confront this difficulty?

In the Initial Stage of group development, the leader is required to mold a group of strangers into a working group using a wide range of skills. What aspects of what you will be called upon to do might be the most exciting? The most difficult?

EXERCISES

1. Analyze each of the following group member statements in terms of role and feeling. Devise an appropriate leader response to the statement and indicate the functions and skills utilized. Remember, these are just for your own practice, so that you will gain some familiarity with the contents of this chapter. It may help you to remember that no absolutely perfect leader response exists.

(a) *Group Member Statement*

I really don't want to spend any more time on career exploration. If Dan needs help with this he should read a book or something. This is supposed to be a group for people who are ready to get into job search full time. I know what I've got to do and I don't want to be held up.

Member Role? Feeling? Unspoken?

Leader Response:

Approach? Skills? Unspoken?

(b) *Group Member Statement*

I really am pleased to hear that I am not the only one who is going through these things. Jill and Mike have had almost identical experiences and the rest of you seem to know what I am saying.

Member Role? Feeling? Unspoken?

Leader Response:

Approach? Skills? Unspoken?

(c) *Group Member Statement*

I wonder if you would mind explaining a little more about what types of back-up resources are available to group members. That's something I really need and I am glad that I may be able to get some help with the costs of photocopying my resumé.

Member Role? Feeling? Unspoken?

Leader Response:

Approach? Skills? Unspoken?

2. Comment on the importance of establishing and making clear group goals and norms in the Initial stage of group development.

3. Describe ways in which the characteristics of the Initial stage influence the selection of structured learning activities for this stage.

Chapter 8

Transition Stage

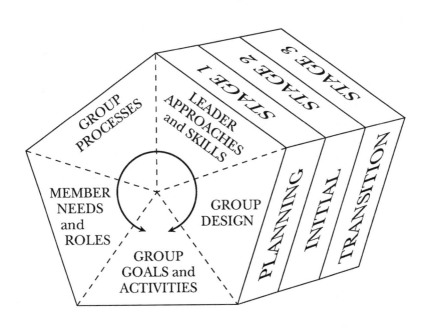

OVERVIEW

In the Initial Stage of group development, members were concerned with finding a place for themselves and being included in the group. Once this "beachhead" has been established, the group moves toward being a productive and efficient means of learning. To achieve this movement, group members must begin to contemplate change and take risks. This process may lead to uneasiness and concern around issues of control and independence which can make people feel reluctant—and their behaviour will reflect this fact.

The process of overcoming reluctance underlies this stage which is called "Transition" because it is a bridge from the Initial Stage to the next stage where the group can be productive and efficient. In varying degrees and at different levels of awareness, this concern with change and risk is present in all clients at the beginning of the Transition Stage.

In Module II terms, this stage is something like the "Re-focus Goal" step with its tie-in to "Build upon Relationship/ Commitment." Almost certainly you will have done the Assessment, clarified goals and elicited client commitment to work on them—but as we know, all these matters can shift and change. True, in large degree, the goals to be achieved—the purposes of the group—have been decided upon before the members were recruited. They are aspects of the goals, notably the changes that will be required of members and the risks involved, which do not become apparent until work is started upon them. It is around these changes and these risks that the real decisions must be made. It is by building on the relationship with the leader (you) and the other members that members find the support and security which provides the courage to take these risks.

If all goes well, by the end of this stage, clients will be ready to come to terms, and grapple with their individual barriers to employment. Hence, the name of the next stage, the Working Stage, which corresponds to the part in Individual Counselling where you assist the client to work on achieving goals (Implement Strategy).

The other major client preoccupation at this stage, not found in such a pronounced form in Module II, is the question of control*. You will recall from an earlier chapter that this concern relates to the individual's need to maintain a sense of control over what happens to him/her and, sometimes, others. When people come together for a group, they initially have a sense of relief and support. Anxiety allayed, the Initial Stage over, is when they start to be uneasy about what is going to happen next in this situation.

It is a little as if, having wanted all your life to learn to swim, you finally sign up for some lessons.

You spend quite a lot of time talking before hand to the instructor, check out the kinds of swim strokes you will learn and other details. When you get to the first class, you find that they are going to make you put your face in the water and keep your eyes open. You don't want to do this. It becomes clear to you that the whole reason you have never learned to swim before is that you are afraid to put your face in the water, especially with your eyes open.

Now you will have a problem with control. You will have to go along with an activity which really worries you to achieve what the lessons offer.

By the end of the Initial Stage, members may understand very clearly the importance of effective job search strategies and the need for self-confidence. As they come to understand the specific activities which they will have to practice such as, for example, telephone techniques or information interviews, they may be inhibited by fear of embarrassment or, what would make matters worse, fear of failure. In discussions of self confidence, they may be afraid to disclose facts such as an inability to sleep at night or stressed family relationships.

A great deal of client behaviour in this, the Transition State, is motivated by uneasiness around the question of control, a desire to get what the group is offering but still have some say in what happens—and trying to find a way for both these things to happen.

---

* Note: Uneasiness about control is often an element of reluctance which is discussed in Module II.

Much client behaviour, as we have seen, will centre around you as leader. Many clients will want you to have perfect, guaranteed answers. This desire, representing dependence, will be offset by the drive for control. Members do not want to be controlled but feel unsure without guidance and hesitant to take the risks they should. The need for members to take risks, the *
dependence vs. independence struggle, the subject of control *
become matters of primary concern for you as leader. *

The processes you concentrate on, the skills you use, the goals you have for the members, the activities you select will all be determined by these overriding client preoccupations.

It is important to note, as you begin reading about this stage, that in structured learning groups, the Transition Stage is frequently quite brief. The nature of the structured learning group provides for the careful selection of activities which promote members' sense of safety and control.

Because leaders are often concerned about possible challenges in this stage, we have described Transition in some detail.

By the end of the Initial Stage, members' inclusion and group cohesion will be underway and individual goals will have been explored and refined.

At this stage you will concentrate your efforts in the following areas:

- developing further group cohesion and trust,

- helping members make a commitment to change, or

- understanding, then challenging members' reluctance to change,

- understanding, then challenging members' reluctance to take risks,

- working with issues of control,

- working with issues of dependence versus independence.

At the completion of this stage you will have brought members to a commitment to change and a readiness to take action in order to achieve their goals.

OBJECTIVES

As a result of reading this chapter, the leader will be competent to:

1. **describe the characteristics of the Transition Stage,**

2. **describe the specific group processes that are prominent in this stage,**

3. **explain how member needs can give rise to certain hindering roles, which will detract from the group's accomplishment and interfere with the development of group maintenance.**

4. **explain how the leader responds to the group in the Transition Stage.**

CHARACTERISTICS OF THE TRANSITION STAGE

As we have indicated, the theme, the issue, most characteristic of this stage is control. A word of explanation. Control is concerned with power, but as the word is used here, it is not a reference to anything so absolute as domination or uniformity but rather, refers to a sort of tension. This tension is intrinsic to a continual process which is usually spread out over a lifetime: how many of our own desires and wishes must we relinquish in order to have, from others, the help, support and affection from the group that we all need? As it is played out in the group, this concern centres on how control is distributed and shared among the members and how the members deal with their individual needs for power.

Uneasiness about power, relative to inclusion, the need to belong (on-going from the Initial Stage) is also experienced by members as a need to feel that they have some influence, that they can contribute to the group. In other words, as people feel a sense of belonging in the group, implying both safety and loyalty, they begin to be aware of the degree to which they are able—or unable—to influence the group, to make a contribution. **Not just**: Am I in? **But**: Do I count? They also begin to notice the degree to which they individually are influenced by the group.

Characteristically, at this stage, then, a rise in tension may be noticed among the members as they begin to feel the push and pull in the group. Some people may be uneasy with the control the leader seems to be exerting (too much or too little) or the degree of control that the agreed-to rules and norms seem to have on them. In early decision making tasks, necessary at this time, members also experience the fact that not everyone agrees with them and when they disagree, they do not even disagree in the same way.

A common source of conflict occurs around who is going to do what, and how and when? As Corey (1985) observes, there is an increase in the number of conversations and discussions about the procedures for decision making and the division of responsibilities. As the struggle around control, and the major member needs which go along, dominate at this stage, differences of opinion are very characteristic.

You will recall that member behaviours and roles arise in the Initial Stage out of the need for inclusion. Similarly, in the Transition Stage, behaviours or roles adopted by members arise from the struggle to resolve their discomfort around the need for control.

Some of the more common ways in which individuals try to handle this struggle are described below:

- Some members attempt to dominate by making decisions for the rest of the group.

- Some withdraw to avoid being controlled by others.
  Resistance to speaking or taking part in certain activities is often a way of controlling. This is called passive control; a way of not letting others dominate.

- A few challenge the group leader, by testing to see how much influence the leader and group members have over the direction of the group. Challenging can also be initiated to test the safety of the group.

Through the process of defining themselves in relation to control, members tend to acquire a greater sense of autonomy or independence. They come to understand that control is not an either/or, all or nothing, proposition and that there is always room for them to make their own decisions and play their own roles. As they are successful in working their way through various situations, a feeling of individuality and uniqueness develops. The same sort of confusion about how to relate to the leader, dependence vs. independence, resolves itself in the same way with the same kind of result.

So that, while this tension, manoeuvering and general restlessness may put you to the test, **it is not in itself a bad thing**—in fact, quite the contrary. The members are moving away from the de- * pendency position characteristic of the Initial Stage to one of as- * suming responsibility for change. *

Satisfactory resolution of the Transition Stage, in other words, how you can tell that the group is ready to move on to the Working Stage, has the following characteristics:

- More activities and functions are beginning to be shared * and spread out over the group, they are no longer * concentrated in the leader. Or conversely, leadership functions are shared and made possible by utilizing all the resources (what each person has to offer) of the group.

- Responsibility for carrying out, and working on projects is * shared. *

- Decision making, especially, using agreed-upon methods for * making decisions is more frequent. *

- Differences of opinion are recognized and accepted among * the members as part of a critical process in the progress of the group, frequently, the members have learned to resolve differences of opinion, or controversy by observing the leader's actions.

- Problems are confronted before they develop into major * conflicts. *

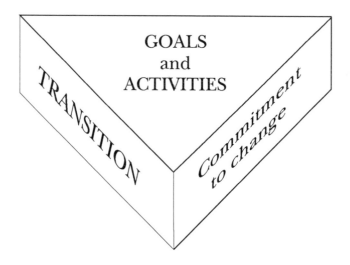

GROUP GOALS AND ACTIVITIES

The Transition Stage is critical, the point where members decide to buy out or buy in. It is the point of ownership of the problem and of acceptance of the need to change. Tension arising from the push and pull of group life has already been described—and to some degree, this push and pull occurs in all groups: groups to form glee clubs or groups to start revolutions. What makes the push and pull here more acute is that it occurs at the same time that the individual member is struggling with the task of accepting responsibility for and ownership of the problem, usually with the (now perceived more accurately than it was in the Assessment interview) "unwelcome" implication that the member must really change. The heightened reluctance which may occur is experienced by the leader and other group members in the hindering roles adopted by uncertain and perplexed participants.

An important goal in the Transition Stage, the sort of thing that you, as leader, know must happen before the group can move on to become effective is that members should commit to and take ownership for what and how they need to change.

How can all this happen?

In order for change and movement even to begin, members need to feel included and secure, goals preferably achieved, or anyway, toward which there has been good progress, in the Initial Stage. Once this initial bonding and cohesiveness begins to grow, the members' trust in the group procedure and in each other begins also to increase dramatically. What happens as a result is that they begin to recognize that many of the feelings and problems they have experienced are similar to the feelings and problems of other members. This feeling of universality, the realization that other people feel the same way, struggle with the same problems, is a powerful release because it relieves people of the idea that they are in some way to blame, or that they are possibly wrong to feel as they do. To put this in everyday terms, the situation is very like a dinner party which does not really get going until people discover a common interest in gardening or the stock market—or a common dislike of, say, a political party. Failure to enjoy this feeling of universality, the kind of inconclusive, floating feeling, the fear of getting stuck with someone with whom one has no interests, or loathings, in common is a prime reason that many people hate cocktail parties!

The development of universality is also one of the great strengths of group counselling. As counsellors, each of us naturally strives to understand our clients and to show that we do. None of us, however, has had every problem and we cannot always have had the same problems as our clients have—and that is often a good thing. When group members recognize the commonality of their problems, the similarity of their reactions and emotions, the feelings that they are OK and normal which this recognition provides are stronger and more credible than any which we, with our emphatic responses, can supply. These member strengths which are present in the group are what you, as leader, will endeavour to tap and make available for members. They are the reason the leader persists in the slightly more complex group situation—because all the helping processes once released, are more powerful.

Members say things like:

"You know Sam, I was beginning to feel as if I was maybe going nuts, you know crazy. But when you said you felt desperate and crazy, I felt relieved, as if I'm OK again."

Agreement is not always absolute. Members recognize that their experiences are also individual and different from those of other members.

"I know my kids are ashamed of me. I wish my family would get behind me and be as great as yours is, Tim!"

Just the same, these people recognize that they have had an experience around a common subject.

This is an example of what you will want to see happening but it may not be a linear development, there is usually some branching. Johnson and Johnson (1982, p. 425) explain that:

> ...in developing close and committed relationships there is first an effort to get to know each other and then often a pulling back in order to differentiate oneself...differentiating is important for group members to establish boundaries where they stop and other members begin and to establish their autonomy as individual and separate members of the group.

Once again, group members do not want to be pushed or controlled. Movement toward a more independent stance away from dependency on the leader also occurs. "That may be good for you, Sue, but for me that would never work," said to a co-member may be paralleled by the same kind of self-differentiating remark to the leader: "I've tried what you said and it didn't help me." For you, as leader, none of this is very worrying. You don't want clones and anyway, everyone is at work on individual, recognized and acknowledged problems.

It is also important to realize that not all this hesitation and, for want of a better word, stubborness, can be attributed to anything so elevated as a need for self-differentiation. Often what underlies this stance is a very common, human "fear of making a fool of myself", looking stupid, dumb. A member with a strong fear of being foolish will defend his/her right to decide even if that decision is to do nothing. After all, if you stand fast, you don't risk a fall! Suggestions from you or another member that it might help to do things differently leave this person untouched. Reluctance may be vocal and vociferous or quiet and passive. "They don't know I really can't do what they're asking. I'll be so embarrassed."

Meanwhile, rising anxiety in another member may be expressed through rebellion against the leader (control, again) or by violating an established group norm, perhaps by putting someone else down.

A good deal of this movement ahead, recognition of a shared problem, will occur of its own volition—even though it might be set about with difficulties, as we have seen. In other words, it is relatively easy for everyone to see the difficulties and the barriers and to feel the profound sense of comradeship which comes from sharing a problem. In World War II, for example, people of London, sheltering from the bombs in the underground railway stations, developed a profound sense of comradeship and mutual caring. Many English people to this day cite these as the happiest times of their lives.

So clearly, in a group situation, comradeship around common problems may easily be the result of having members discuss their difficulties in the Initial Stage. The challenge for you is to move them from where they can only see problems to where they can see options and possibilities. Without question you are already familiar with members' real fears: that they will never work again, that they will have to accept a much reduced income, become "poor", that they may have to change careers. When we said, at the beginning of this section, that this stage is critical, what we meant is: either members re-focus and see an opportunity now or they remain discouraged, and stuck, glued to something that experience has shown does not function, and afraid to try anything new. Your intuitive sense of timing for each member, the way you carefully carefully balance confronting with empathy, the activities you may decide to introduce to promote trust and self-disclosure are all key. An attitude of warmth, caring and hope also provides support in this time of turmoil. All these skills you learned in Modules I and II and they remain the essential tools of the trade, modified slightly to fit into the group setting. They will be reviewed in the training workshop.

Once the members begin to see the possibilities rather than the barriers, movement through this stage can be relatively quick.

In terms of the Group Goals for this stage, how precisely, with what exactitude, must they be achieved? To take the second one first: that members should commit to and take responsibility for assisting other members in their change process, much of this is implicit in the increased levels of self-disclosure, levels of interpersonal trust, functions being shared and so on described above. It is not that one might expect any sort of "one for all and all for one" kind of compact but there will be a give-and-take of feedback which is easy and unanxious, some reaching out, demonstrations of concern and helpfulness. Not everyone will perform all this at the same level but its existence among some people will be perceptible to you.

In terms of the first Group Goal, that members should commit to and take ownership for what and how they have to change, the same unevenness should be expected. Obviously, members will not move in lockstep to come to a neat halt when they have achieved this goal. What you need, what is essential, is that at least a few members move toward acceptance of responsibility, enough to swing most to the point where there is group commitment to responsibility for change, acceptance of group goals and procedures and the commitment to each other. When this swing occurs, in however ragged a way that it might—to repeat, you will not be reminded of the Rockettes when it does—the group can move on to productive achievement of its goals and purposes.

Figure 4 helps to illustrate the nature of the Transition Stage as the central turning point in the life of the group and the evolution in commitment to goals by group members.

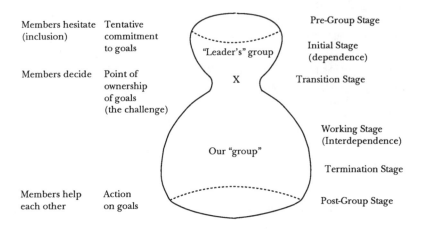

Members hesitate (inclusion) — Tentative commitment to goals — "Leader's" group — Pre-Group Stage

Initial Stage (dependence)

Members decide — Point of ownership of goals (the challenge) — X — Transition Stage

Working Stage (Interdependence)

Our "group"

Termination Stage

Members help each other — Action on goals — Post-Group Stage

MEMBER NEEDS AND ROLES

Here are your group members, starting Transition, feeling, already, uneasy, tense and, very likely, a little helpless. Now you *
are going to ask them to give up some control—in which resides *
their sense of security—take some risks and some pretty big leaps *
of trust toward other group members. You may see some reluc- *
tance.

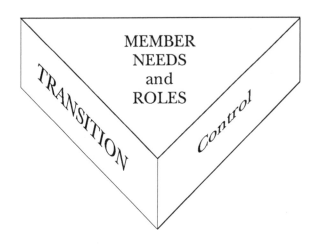

MEMBER NEEDS and ROLES

TRANSITION

Control

As members deal with control and security issues, their uneasi- *
ness more or less ensures that a greater emphasis upon hinder- *
ing roles occurs. The hindering actions of Dominating, With- *
drawing and Grandstanding described in the Initial Stage of
group development (Chapter VII) may still be present. In addition, two new roles, Stone-walling and Negating, may emerge.

Stone-waller
Holding up the group's work or progress by sticking to an idea
or position; repeatedly rejecting the ideas of others; returning
over and over again to one's own ideas and suggestions.

Negator
Disagreeing repeatedly with ideas and suggestions of others; trying to prove that nothing will work; challenging for the sake of
challenging.

Example:

"Employers hire people they know. It's as simple as that.
There is no point in working at developing better interview
techniques. You're just wasting your time."

"I don't think there is any point looking at different career
options since there just aren't any jobs available. I know
from my own experience that it is just a waste of time. I
know I'm probably beginning to sound like a broken
record, but I feel strongly about this."

It will be apparent that these roles share a common refusal to *
move, to abandon control and, above all, to take a risk—a stance *
reflecting members' fears of embarrassment and possible failure *
when they try something new. *

It is not the case, however, that you will meet a solid wall of
opposition. More helpful roles: Information and Opinion
Seeker, Harmonizer, Tension Reliever and Encourager are vital
and do continue to appear as members successfully challenge
their own and other people's fears.

Your major preoccupation, however, is with the tension that
some group members may feel as they consider the degree to
which they are willing to discuss their own situations, to help
others, to accept responsibility for, and commitment to change.

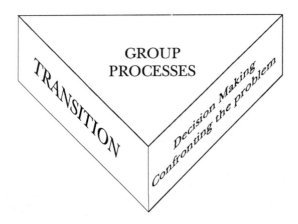

GROUP PROCESSES

It will be evident that the group processes, in which concerns about control and risk-taking are embedded like nerve endings in human muscle, will not remain untouched or unmoved at this stage. It is important that processes develop, in fact the group cannot exist or function without them but, again, some of this development also generates discomfort.

The situation is a little like the one where a coach is training an athlete. To win, the athlete must have muscle, speed, visual acuity and judgment. The coach works to bring out all these needed qualities but building them is accompanied by doubts and fatigue—as well as high hopes—and all of these feelings affect muscle, speed, visual acuity and performance.

A crucial process for the group at this stage, for example, is decision making—its potential for provoking tension in relation to control and risk-taking ("Are they going to decide something I don't want to do?", "I'm sure I can't do that") is also obvious.

The key group processes with which the group and the leader must contend at this point are:

1. communication,

2. norms,

3. decision-making,

4. confronting the problem.

Communication

The communication skills you might use remain technically always the same: a paraphrase is a paraphrase, empathy is empathy, unchanged in Module I or II, at the office party or in conversation with a friend. Your objectives vary according to circumstances.

At this point in group development, you are trying to use communication to encourage further cohesiveness and also member self-disclosure (which will appear more readily in the Working Stage). In addition, it is also important to try to make everyone feel valued and important and to establish some norms for effective communication. All these goals, achieved or in the process of being achieved are related in an important way to rendering member strength available to the group and to increasing the flow of information. People who feel valued and respected, who know they will be listened to, share what they have (people who don't, won't).

Key communication skills, then, at this stage are empathy and confronting (or challenging). Empathy you will use to show concern and caring, to make people feel valued and important, to build a supportive climate. Confronting is important, judiciously used (and you will recall from Module II, this is not a skill to be used on first acquaintance), in order to challenge members with their strengths to help consolidate a move into action.

Consider the following examples of empathy and confronting used to diffuse the hindering roles typical of this stage.

Examples

Blocking:
Sometimes, people talk too much, they interrupt and seem unaware that other people have something to say. You cannot allow this situation to continue but you still need the talker to make input (as needed) and feel valued. In fact, you accomplish these goals in reverse order: first make the person feel recognized and valued, then move in with your message.

Example:

Member. (Interrupts Bill, another group member...): "Yes, that happened to me too, but you see, if you only..."

You take these steps:

Recognition:

Not so important in individual counselling where the client is the only one you could be talking to, but obviously very important in group, especially at the beginning. It is a good idea to use the name, just to show you are aware of each person. (Later, names may not be important).

> "You seem really excited,
>
> Marvin,

Empathy:

show that you understand, accept and approve, you know the impulse is a good one

> I know that this is very important to you and you share Bill's ideas.

Here's the message.

> When you interrupt, we can't hear Bill's ideas."

You can see that empathy is used in Recognition ("You seem really excited...") and that the empathy is also important to make Marvin feel valued. Both recognition and empathy are used in the blocking statements to enhance group strengths.

Linking:

There are some behaviours you want to encourage. Sometimes you want to show members that they are relating to each other and working together and show them what they have in common.

The three steps:

Recognition

the name	"Sylvia
Sue's name— you recognize her, too	I like the way you listened to Sue and caught the key piece of information to clarify back to her.

Immediacy:

not between you and the client but what you have noticed between member and member. (Note also: recognition of "our group.")	"I have been noticing this happening a lot in ou group.
Here's the message.	It helps members to feel valued and that their point of view is important."

In these examples, ordinary communication skills: Paraphrasing, Empathy, Confronting are used with a special recognition of the group setting. The client is first recognized, a move hardly necessary when there are only two people present, and the skill is used to help people feel "OK" so that you can promote (or discourage) behaviour needed (or not wanted) in the group setting. Equally important, you have modelled the sort of accepting, valuing communication that you want group members to use.

Use of communication skills to develop good group process does not mean, of course, that you will never, in group, use Empathy, Confronting or any other skill in the more traditional way to heighten a member's individual self-awareness.

Norms

The norms for the Transition Stage are the same as they are in the Initial Stage—and, in fact, ideally, what they are throughout the life of the group. What is different is that now members are beginning to internalize them. Up until now you have had to take care to describe and model them. Now is when the results of *
your efforts begin to appear. What this means is that members' *
ways of relating to each other are closer to what you are hoping *
for. They also model for each other and if monitoring or guid- *
ance is needed it will be done, quite often, by them. *

As an example, a member who has internalized the norm about not interrupting may say: "Sam, each person has to be heard". Here, the member recognized the speaker and certainly gave the message, which embodied the norm, very clearly. You would probably have taken more care to show Sam that you understood and accepted him. At this point it would be for you to judge whether you might like to break Sam's fall a little for him by making a remark. for example, about his enthusiasm or the quality of his contributions. Possibly, you might like to help the Blocker's strategy a little: "You're right to remember the rule, Mustapha. Sam, you're bursting with an idea. Maybe you could share it when the others finish."

By the end of the Transition, some people may have internalized norms so well that they block as carefully as you do. "I can tell you are excited! Hang on, until Christie is finished!" Speaking in this manner probably indicates, also, that there is a high level of trust in the group.

Decision Making

It is easy to understand that more than anything, members are concerned with the work the group is going to do: not, primarily, to develop wonderful group skills—essential as we know them to be—but to *do* things that will help them get jobs. What these things should be and how members will do them, or learn to do them, can all be matters for contention and the familiar problems of control and risk-taking may arise. Ways of making deci- *
sions and the development of decision making skills are crucial *
at this stage, critical to whether the work of the group gets done. *

Groups will sometimes have difficulty in decision making simply because people do not always agree and some people simply will not go along with the view of the group. Clearly, if people feel they have been forced, then bad feelings may arise and members will not feel "safe", for example, in performing a job interview practice for feedback and correction. We know that at this time members may already have a lot of concern about making a career switch, facing a lower salary or generally making a commitment to change. So this is a situation where you might expect to see some "passive control": people avoiding fear by simply opting out of an "agreed-upon", structured activity. "I know it might help me, but Judy told me she did not videotape and her interview was successful." Possibly this person is also concerned about looking foolish.

Decisions can be made in the group in several ways; some are generally more useful than others but none is invariably correct. They can be made:

- by the leader,

- by a single member who has enough power to influence others or railroad it through,

- by a minority of the members, without consultation with the majority,

- through a majority of the members agreeing by voting or secret balloting,

- through general agreement of all group members— consensus.

Decision making pushed through by a powerful individual or the leader has its advantages. It is quick and, at least superficially, appears efficient. Disadvantages occur as well. All the information needed for a "good" decision may not be available to the members and, in any case, individuals not having a voice are unlikely to be motivated or committed to making the decision work.

Majority or minority rule certainly has more to offer the decision making process. Both allow for more member commitment to an action and the decision, having had input from a wider range, will be superior. **But**, voting has its disadvantages. Members who wanted a different decision are probably unhappy and will, at times, actively work (as in the case of the person who did not want to be videotaped) to sabotage the decision. In many countries of the world, for example, the people who lose elections worry a lot about the kind of control the winners will impose. Their only recourse, as they see it, is to take to the hills with supplies of guns and ammunition from where they conduct destructive raids on the efforts of the governing group. In a figurative sense, people in the minority in a vote often behave in the same way. Exactly as in the case of many struggling governments, a lot of the group's energy may be wasted and fragmentation of goals can occur. In short, there is a winner and loser with all that that implies. Voting sets up competition and constitutes an occasion ripe for argumentation and conflict among members and/or with the leader.

A decision does not have to be win-lose. Effective decision-making should result in a solution which all agree on and support. The search, in otherwords, is for consensus. Individual needs, expertise and resources members have at their disposal are all considered in arriving at the solution.

The preoccupation with control is always centred at this time * on the way decisions are made. Members want to be sure that * they are being heard, have a voice and can disagree without fear of being rejected (all this was described in "Characteristics...." at the beginning of this Chapter). Decision making by arriving at * consensus prevents the control issue from becoming negative or * turning into active conflict. Power is distributed equally to mem- * bers and influence does not become a source of conflict. This process can help to consolidate members' commitment to a decision and can swing people into action.

Reaching consensus on all decisions can be very time consuming, essentially unnecessary, and perhaps not productive. It is important for key decisions. Equally, you need to be aware of when the diminishing gains outweigh productivity and consensus is not necessary—some decisions are trivial and unlikely to bother people either way.

Very often, members will not have a very good idea of how to go about reaching consensus. Don't be afraid to give a little nudge, push or pull. Here are some suggestions. They are to give you an idea. It is **not** necessary to memorize them.

Helpful Leader Behaviours
for Establishing Effective Decision Making

1. Structure activities for group centred learning in a form that encourages (or, maybe, obliges) members to work toward consensus (more about this subject later in the chapter). For example, you might say, "Come to an agreement as a group on what decision you should make. Attempt to arrive at a decision all members of your group can support." This is a reminder to members that all points of view should be considered.

2. When the group arrives at a decision, check to see if it really is consensus. For example, "Jim, you were not sure about this decision before the discussion. Tell me how you feel about it now." Note the open question. Asking "Are you feeling OK now?", for example, may push polite members to express an acquiescence they do not have. You need to find out in this stage if all members, especially those with differing opinions, are listened to and quiet ones encouraged to share opinions. Sometimes you may help the group to overcome the obstacles which are interfering with consensus. Or you might try some Confronting: "Saraya, you seem a little reluctant!"

3. Do not push for a quick and artificial consensus. Members may want to please you and others by pretending that they agree. When a group opts for consensus, the idea is definitely not to get everyone to agree to sign on the dotted line.

4. Help members understand that consensus can be achieved in many ways:

    a) one side persuades the other;
    b) one side gives in;

c) both sides find new alternatives;
d) the group redefines the issues;
e) each side gives in a little;
f) both sides agree to let it ride.

5. Offer suggestions for how members can be helpful to the group in its decision-making. Point out that they should:

a) "Concentrate on the content, what the other person is saying. This isn't to say you can't state your position. Remember, it's when the irritation gets into your voice that everything goes sour!";

b) "Strive for win-win situations; something for everyone!";

c) "Be willing to change your mind.";

d) "Try to listen to other points of view.";

e) "View differences of opinion as natural, helpful, and energizing."

6. Model consensus-seeking behaviour whenever you reasonably can.

Confronting the Problem

So far, we have examined three processes which are important to movement through the Transition Stage: good communication, norm maintenance and decision-making. A fourth group involves confronting problems so they are not suppressed or ignored only to explode into open conflagration later.

A skilled leader takes a proactive stance in anticipating the possibility of dealing with problems in the Transition Stage—and then deals with them before they get out of proportion and present enormous problems. If you ignore or avoid a problem—whether it is a difference of opinion between two members, one individual who insists on dominating in the decision making procedures, or the whole group engaging in resistant behaviour—the problem will not simply go away, however fervently you may wish it would. It simmers, intensifies and continues to plague every activity. It distracts the group from its work and drains the members emotionally. It may erupt into a full-blown conflict. Stanford (1977, p. 201) says:

> Unless members and "the leader" are willing to confront and learn from their problems, there is little hope that the group can improve its functioning... Most of us have the impulse to avoid confronting interpersonal problems because we're uncomfortable handling the tensions that confrontation might produce.

In a "good" confrontation, you will help the group to deal with the problem. You do this by communicating directly about, and with those involved. And you do not allow members to avoid the issue. With this kind of open and direct approach, a resolution becomes possible.

Some suggestions for confronting the problem follow. Other suggestions will come in your training.

A.   Observe the group and give feedback if you suspect a problem. Feedback could take the form of a description of what you see—or what you feel. (You have been Process Observing.)

Leader: "The group seems to be bogged down. Could someone here say what they think is happening? Perhaps if we can take a look at what is going on, we can find out if we want to go about this another way or do something else."

The leader brings the problem(s) to the group's attention and proceeds to help the group facilitate analysis and resolution. Always work toward making what is covert, overt and focus attention on the situation not the individual's personality. As another illustration, consider the following:

Leader: "The group seems restless! You don't seem to want to settle down!" (The Problem). "Is there something worrying/difficult about what we're doing" (Facilitate Analysis). "Should we take another look at why we're doing this? Did we make a wrong decision? Should we try and decide again?" (Try for Resolution).

B.   Here are our modified versions of suggestions presented by Stanford (1977, p. 205) for focusing on the problem.

1. Invite group members to describe their behaviour—which you, and maybe the rest of the group, regard as a "problem"—before you give them your perceptions of it. If people can identify their own problems, they are much more likely to try to be honest than if you—or anyone else—points them out, which often suggests criticism. Hold back from offering your diagnosis. For example, rather than saying "This discussion was not successful because you didn't stay on the topic", try to get them to analyze matters themselves. Ask "How well were you able to meet your goal?", "Is there anything you would like to change?" or even "How well did you stay on topic?"

2. If you must give your own perceptions, describe specific behaviour and avoid abstract analyses. For example, "Marcel, you and Ted sat apart from the group and spoke only when someone else asked you a question" is more helpful than "Marcel, you and Ted weren't involved."

3. Check the accuracy of your perceptions by asking whether the group members see their behaviour as you did.

4. Avoid words that imply a judgment. Let the group evaluate whether the behaviour you have observed is good (i.e., helpful in reaching the goal) or not. Don't say "Today's discussion was not what I would have expected of you ...." A better approach would be: "We're having a lot of interruptions today. How is that working for us?", or "What effect do you think these interruptions had on the discussion?"

5. Focus on behaviour the group can do something about, not on factors beyond its control. "Is this something I can logically and reasonably expect this group to be able to correct or change?" If the answer is "no", don't burden them with it. You may, for example, reasonably expect members to arrive at an agreed-upon time. If members persist in coming late, then this is a situation you must confront. If the group is composed of individuals from a culture where submissiveness is valued, you cannot expect that assertiveness will come easily or be handled well; innovative or creative propositions may be expressed by group members, but probably not often. You cannot, after all, ask people to give what they do not possess or to do what they do not have it in them to do. To say all this is not to say that you should accept every bad or regrettable thing you may encounter, only to realize that there is a limit to what you can do in the time at your disposal—and that there are also limits to your legitimate mandate within a CEC setting. And that there is no point in stressing your clients more than is necessary.

6. Ask members of the group to repeat, paraphrase, or summarize the behaviour you described in order to determine whether you have communicated clearly.

7. To confront:

a) Describe what you see happening, the symptoms of the trouble you think (but are not sure) may be brewing.

"Doug, you and Loren sat apart from the group and spoke only when someone else asked you a question."

"We're having a lot of interruptions today."

"People are taking a long time settling down to this project."

"Marcel and Ted have argued on opposite sides from each other several items this morning."

b) Play it safe. Check with other members including, if you are talking to a particular member, that member her (or him) self.

> "Am I off base?"
>
> "Did it look that way to you, Swinder?"
>
> "Can you tell me exactly what happened?"
>
> "Did anyone else notice that?"
>
> "I am wondering if the group saw that or was it just me?"

If you are off base, you might as well admit your mistake. That, too, is good modeling.

c) Check that people heard you right.

> "Am I being clear? What did it sound as if I said?"
>
> "Am I right? Tell me what you hear me saying."

d) Don't say the thing that hurts: the diagnoses, the analyses, the judgments—and remember all of these implied judgments can also be in your voice tone, body posture or eyes, even if your words stick to a bare description of behaviour. These are the statements that imply disapproval, that provoke anger, that fester and get you into trouble. The reason many people avoid confrontation is because they think it must make use of the derogatory, but it need not.

e) Let your voice assume that members had a good reason to behave as they did. Keep the ball in the member's (or members') court, ask:

"When this happens (the behaviour), how do things go?"

"If there is a problem, why do you think it happened?"

"Do you think we should be trying a different way?"

C. Teach the group to be process observers and then assign responsibility for monitoring the group process to the members themselves—the same kind of approach you used when you ask individual group members to describe their behaviour. Ask them to observe what facilitates and what hinders the work. You can use structured activities or questionnaires to teach these skills, to give practice in observing and recording what has been observed. You did very much the same thing in Module II when you taught clients to observe. Here, you must take extra care not to use procedures which are threatening; you want to be sure that observations by some members do not leave others feeling crushed and negative.

What to Watch Out For in Group Processes:

The points listed below are not absolutely identical to all the skills just studied—they do constitute valid indicators, however, a checklist of what to watch out for! The idea is not to check for perfection but to check where things might be better.

Communication. Did people feel free to talk and say what was really on their minds? Was there a great deal of interrupting or cutting people off? Did people listen to others? Was there clarification of points made? Did people look at whomever they were talking to or did they look somewhere else, the table, or still too often, at you, the leader? Was there any attempt to summarize and pull together various ideas? Did people try to clarify and interpret suggestions and ideas?

Norms. The kind of implicit group norms which the leader should be monitoring are: Were members sensitive to each other's needs and concerns? Did everyone have opportunities to participate? Were some individuals excluded? Was an effort made to draw people out? Was everyone participating or did a few of the members do most of the talking?

You may recall that these are the norms which you endeavour to establish by modeling rather than by discussion. If the implicit norms are not what you have been hoping for, it will certainly be helpful to look at your own role.

Decision-Making. Did the group get a lot of ideas (brainstorm) before beginning to decide, or did it begin deciding with only a single idea? When an idea or suggestion was presented to the group, was it immediately evaluated and explored further or dropped? Did everyone agree to the decisions made? Who helped influence decisions of others? Who supported other members' suggestions or decisions? Does this support result in a few members deciding the topic or activity for the group (an "in" group, an élite)? How does this situation affect other group members? Is there any evidence of a majority pushing a decision through over other members' objections (railroading)? Do majority members call for a vote (majority support)? Is there any attempt to get all members participating in a decision (consensus)? What effect does this seem to have on the group? In short, did anything occur which was seriously out-of-line with consensus?

Confronting the Problem. Who initiated ideas? Were they support-ed? And by whom? Did anyone block? Who helped push for deci-sions? And if they pushed too hard, is there a rebellion brewing? Does it happen that someone may ask for or make suggestions as to the best way to proceed or to tackle a problem and then not receive any kind of response or recognition (plop)? What effect does this have on the member? (Resentment on the simmer?) Does anyone make a decision and carry it out without checking with other group members? (For example, a member decides on the topic to be discussed and immediately begins to talk about it.) What effect does this have on other group members? (This is the self-authorized, self-styled aristocrat—better stop him/her before the group goes for the guillotine!). Does the group drift from topic to topic? Who jumps topics? Can you discern a reason for this aimlessness in the way the group members interact? Are they hiding from you? Or from themselves? Anything else that is worrying you?

If you are feeling uneasy, check out the source of the discomfort.

* * * * * * * * * *

Groups where the processes are poor simply do not go anywhere! If these processes are cultivated and begin to take hold and grow, the group will move more efficiently through the Transition Stage into the Working Stage of group development.

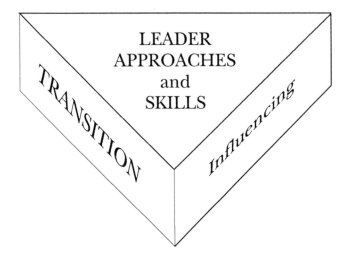

LEADER APPROACHES AND SKILLS

By now it will be clear to you that your job is to build a bridge over these possibly troubled waters.

Members are just beginning to realize that the group's goals are going to require a high level of commitment, work, trust and action and all of these requirements are related in a worrying way to the questions of control, risk and dependence *vs.* independence. It is not surprising that they may experience some reluctance and, in fact, their behaviour, the roles they choose, reflect this fact. By contrast, they want a way out of their problems,

they want what the group offers. As leader, you are challenged to   *
deal with this kind of approach-withdrawal attitude.   *

Keep in mind that:

- members need to maintain some sense of control regarding
  their level of participation and, naturally also, over the goals
  they are to achieve;

- you need to be sensitive to member concerns and anxieties, in
  whichever way they may be expressed. Sometimes, for example,
  people say, "I'm not sure this group is for me!" while others
  arrive late or simply stay away. All this member tension also
  shows up, very characteristically, at this stage in the form of
  hindering roles. "You need to be sensitive..." means, in
  practical terms, that "You need to watch out for trouble";

- you are going to use your leader skills to best advantage   *
  particularly, to challenge, confront and support, to move   *
  members from where they are to where they need to be, to   *
  help them see over the barriers to the possibilities, to help   *
  them take risks and move out to a new independence.   *

At this point, you will be drawing heavily upon the Influencing   *
approach in order to: *

- manage the interactions in ways which enable members to   *
  cope with their own reluctance (you may have people observe   *
  their own behaviour as we described in the confrontation   *
  process, for example);   *

- present ways for the group to make decisions necessary to   *
  arrive at agreed-upon goals (see: the Decision-making process,   *
  earlier in this chapter);   *

- assist members to find their own roles and places in the group   *
  in terms of the degree of self-versus-other control (all the   *
  process categories are good for this, structured activities, too);   *

- guide the group members to a point where they begin to   *
  accomplish tasks on their ownwithout depending on you.   *

Here, once more, are the member statements provided earlier in the "member needs and roles" section. These statements reflect two hindering roles not illustrated in the Initial Stage which are particularly characteristic of the Transition Stage. For each example, the member's statement is provided along with the identified member role, possible member feelings and a leader response. In addition, the leader response is categorized according to the skills which are used.

Member Statement

"I don't think there is any point in looking at different career options since there just aren't any jobs available. I know from my experience that it is just a waste of time. I know I'm probably beginning to sound like a broken record, but I feel strongly about this."

Role:	Stone-waller.
Feeling:	Discouraged, frustrated, hopeless.
Unspoken:	"Everywhere I look, I get discouraged. There's no point in changing and, anyhow, I don't want to!"

Leader Response

"You seem to feel really 'boxed-in'. In some ways it seems useless to look at different career options, and you know that there aren't many prospects in your current line. Al (another group member) has said that it worries him to look at other options because he may not have the skills. I wonder if this kind of kind of concern is troubling you also? What do you think?"

Skills:	Empathy, Reframing, Rephrasing, Confrontation, Linking, Open-ended Question.
Unspoken:	"I know you're feeling frustrated and panicky! You don't want to change but there doesn't seem much alternative. It's OK to have the feeling you have, other people do."

Here, you have used empathy, confrontation, etc. and then linking. You are helping the member to deal with her or his own reluctance by linking an emotion, fear, to the same emotion in another member. You are, in fact, helping to establish Universality. It is much more powerful to understand that Al, right there in the same room, is also afraid, than it would be be to accept your private and personal assurance that other people —"somewhere out there"—also have the same fear.

Member Statement

"Employers hire people they know. It's as simple as that. There's no point in working at developing better interview techniques. You're just wasting your time."

Role:	Negator.
Feeling:	Helpless, angry, cynical, frustrated.
Unspoken:	"Don't tell me! I know! I'm not going to let you get my hopes up because I don't want to deal with the disappointment."

Leader Response

"The whole system seems to be against you. You feel really frustrated and angry with your lack of success in finding work. If employers hire people they know there seems to be little hope for you and yet, other people in the group seem to have had some promising prospects turn up. I wonder if some other people would tell us some of what their experiences have been."

Skills:	Empathy, Reframing, Open-ended question, Confronting.
Unspoken:	"I hear your worry and fear! I know it's going to cost to try again! Let's take a small, first step!"

Here, confronting is used to deal with reluctance and it is very powerful when linked with the experiences of other members. This is an example of one of the advantages of group counselling.

The illustrations above provided focus on the hindering roles of Stonewaller and Negator. The other hindering roles which also are prevalent at the Transition State include Dominater, Withdrawer and Grandstander, all terrific roles for members who want to avoid dealing with what is going on. These roles were introduced in the previous chapter (the Initial Stage) along with examples of appropriate leader responses.

In addition to the illustrations which have been provided, we attach a list of practical leader suggestions.

Practical Leader Suggestions for the Transition Stage

1.   Be alert: watch out for trouble.

   • Don't avoid negative group member behaviour, it will
     only get worse. Confront the problem openly,
     non-judgmentally, using Empathy and Paraphrasing.
     (See: Confronting the Problem).

   • Pick up on the negative undercurrents as well as the
     more obvious conflicts. That is, pay attention to voice
     tone, body language and passive resistance.

   • Be a close observer of structured activities. This
     observation keeps you current in your knowledge of how
     members are behaving and whether they are getting
     anything out of the group.

   • If members are persisting in negative behaviour, talk
     about it openly in the group and, if necessary, on an indi-
     vidual basis.

2.   Model the behaviour you want members to adopt.

   • Model the behaviour and attitudinal qualities of respect,
     hope and openness that you expect from others. If you
     make it OK (and non-threatening) to talk about anxiety
     or hostility (for example), it will be.

3. Reinforce the behaviour you want members to adopt.

- Reinforce those members who are resolving conflict in a positive fashion.

- Reinforce those members who are engaging in positive task and maintenance actions.

4. Stay positive.

- Help members to rethink their fears and concerns into constructive action possibilities.

5. Stay sensitive to your own input.

- Be aware of your own reactions to members' hindering behaviours. This sensitivity and awareness can prevent you from falling into a trap where you become part of the problem, the one the members feel obliged to hinder!

- Understand that during the Transition Stage, group members may not always be positive about you, other members, or the group generally. As we have seen, the tendency may be in quite the opposite direction. You must try to recognize the difference between a challenge arising from this stage of development and an attack on your leadership.

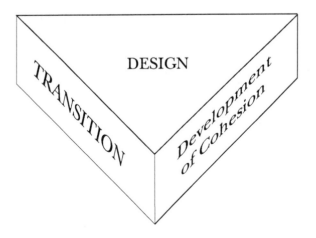

DESIGN

Activities designed for the Transition Stage of group development are selected to continue to build the trust and inclusion of
members begun in the Initial Stage but now on a more substan-
tial level. The trust and inclusion serve as spring boards for the
plunge into risk-taking which will be important at this stage.

As the "getting to know you" period comes to a close, members may begin to disclose more about the issues really concerning them. The tension (Did I go too far? Wil they understand?
Think I'm a nerd?) that they may feel as a result can cause them
to beat a retreat and/or resist disclosing any more—a sort of
"one step forward, two steps back" process. Activities you may design need to push for some forward progress, to nudge members
into risking/trusting more and, therefore, into confronting the
fear/resistance that may be engendered. Implementing these activities, which are complex and require skill, will probably engender additional pressure for you. You need also to provide activities which will induce members to begin to establish for
themselves ways to make decisions and confront problems (important group processes) and lay a foundation for action. This
necessity and the abiding worry about control will require you to
help members to understand how to make decisions in such a
way that they feel they have had direction or influence in the
group and, at the same time, to accept that the group will, from
time to time, have influence or control over them: the quintessential issue of control.

Specific Transition Design Issues

Activities for this stage would ideally:

- involve members in completing an activity which requires
  them to "give and take" on specific questions, issues, or
  beliefs, etc.;

- provide guidelines, modeling, demonstrations of, or
  procedures for making these decisions (process);

- arrange for the group to make decisions "as a group" so that the members experience and observe good ways in which decisions are, or can be, made;

- provide an opportunity for the group to identify and evaluate effective decision-making styles for different types of problems;
- utilize the communication skills which promote effective confrontation of problems and a reduction in defensiveness;
- recognize the behaviour or roles of members which facilitated or hindered decision-making;
- recognize career/lifestyle changes that may be necessary in reaching goals.

Example of a Structured Design Activity

The following pages contain an example of a specific activity which illustrates several of the issues of the Transition Stage.

TITLE: OPPORTUNITY KNOCKS

Time Required : 72 minutes

Goals

1. To have members recognize how each member brings different ideas to a specific situation.
2. To introduce the decision making process for job search.
3. To show that there is a variety of good decisions that can be made.
4. To help members evaluate the pros and cons of each solution.
5. To make members aware of group norms, communication style, confronting differences of opinion and methods of giving feedback.

Group Size

> small group (4–5); large group

Materials

> paper, pencil, Opportunity Knocks Forms (see page 190)

Physical Setting

> large room

Description of Activity:

This activity helps the client clarify his/her decision-making process during the job search. This activity is a large group activity.

Procedure: (How you do it):

1. Members are divided into groups of 4–5 (sub-groups)—2 mins.

2. Introduce activity—2 min.:

Opportunity Knocks

Suppose that you are interested in a job as a waiter in a particular restaurant. This is highly sought after position because of the management of the restaurant and the money which can be made in tips.

As you are passing by you meet someone you know who is working at the restaurant. He tells you that they will be needing someone to fill in for a couple of weeks as the person they were using for temporary replacement is getting married. When you look at the restaurant you see the manager put a "Help Wanted" sign in the window. Your friend tells you that he doesn't know how long that will last. A lot of people are interested in getting their foot in the door.

What do you do? You have a resumé in your car, but your car is 10 blocks away. You are dressed in shorts and a T-shirt If you go home and change it will take at least an hour to get back to the restaurant.

3. Distribute "Opportunity Knocks" Design Form.

4. Members brainstorm ideas about viability of each option and develop additional options (a recorder/spokesperson is appointed by the group)—15 min.

5. A consensus is reached—10 mins.

6. Spokesperson for each group reports to the large group the decision of their sub-group—5 min.

7. Leader promotes a discussion on the following topics:

   (a) the whole range or variety of decisions

   (b) whether there was one "good decision" to be made in the situation—10 min.

8. Leader instructs sub-groups to process their own decision-making process giving each other specific feedback (use feedback rules)—15 min.

9. Leader debriefs this in large group—10 min.

10. Leader summarizes—3 min.

Opportunity Knocks Decision Form

You need to come to a consensus *as a group* on which is the best option and then rank order the remaining options. Feel free to develop additional options if necessary.

Option 1. You go home, get changed, and return to the restaurant with your resumé.

Option 2. You run back to your car and get your resumé, then return to the restaurant.

Option 3. You enter the restaurant and talk to the manager about the job.

Option 4. You go home and telephone the manager to set up an appointment.

Option 5. (To be developed by group members.)

POINTS TO REMEMBER

The Transition Stage is the turning point where the movement from concentration on the barriers to concentrating on the possibilities occurs. During this stage, members assume responsibility and ownership for the need to change and, as a result, commit themselves to action. The goals of the group change hands moving from the several originators, the leader and individual members to become the property of the group as a whole. This change occurs as the participants begin to perceive membership in the group as a positive vehicle for goal achievement but one which must be fueled by their own efforts.

The following points have been important in this chapter.

- Leader goals involve maintaining an atmosphere of safety (build inclusion and trust) and providing the stimulus and challenge for group members to risk change and become independent.

- Member goals are to own responsibility for the problem(s) they face and to commit to change.

- The key needs of members are to maintain a sense of control over their own goals and to commit to the goals of the group.

- Group processes are communication, norm enforcement, decision-making and confronting problems.

- The leader's approach is geared to facilitate interaction and to challenge members to commit to action using primary and advanced empathy, paraphrasing, confrontation, linking, supporting, blocking, confronting and immediacy.

POINTS TO PONDER

The Transition Stage has been characterized as one in which group members may react negatively as a result of feeling pressure to change. Think about how *you* may respond to these hindering actions and how you can handle your own feelings of anxiety and threat.

The Transition Stage has been described as a "bottle neck" point of decision regarding commitment to goals that may require change. This process, while a necessary forerunner to the productive Working Stage, may seem to slow down movement of the group towards reaching its goals. How do you think you will react to this "slow down"? What feelings will *you* need to contend with?

EXERCISES

Evaluate each of the following three dialogue segments in terms of member needs and roles and leader approaches and skills. Suggest alternate leader approaches and/or skills which could have been used.

Remember that in group counselling there is rarely one, absolutely perfect, counsellor response; usually there are several accept-able replies which one might reasonably make. So the purpose of these exercises is to have you think about what you might want to accomplish and which skills you might use. Do your best but do not worry about having the correct answer—no one could say whether you have or haven't.

Setting: Career exploration group for young adults.
                Second session.

Characters: **Leader:**   Mary: pleased with initial session
                                and now wants to begin by
                                having group members explore
                                their interests.

              Group Members: Joe, Mike, Fred, Diane, Jules and
                                Simone.

Dialogue #1

Leader: I was very pleased about how things went yesterday and
(Mary)   I'm excited about the progress we are making. I would
          like to start today by having you break into pairs and
          then look more closely at your interests, I think that ...
          (interruption)

Joe: I don't see why we're starting with interests. In today's job market all I want to know is where the jobs are.

Mary: I can appreciate your concern about the job market, maybe we should start with that.

Joe: I really would like you, as the job expert, to tell us what are the best fields.

Mary: Well, I do have some ideas, but I would like to first hear from you about what you think are the best fields.

Diane: Don't ask me, I don't know what's available out there. As far as I can see, it's only a matter of who you know.

Mary: OK, let me give you some ideas. Here is some information from the Department of Labour...

Dialogue #1

| | Member | | | Leader | |
	Needs	Role		Approach	Skills
Joe			Used		
Dianne			Alternate		

Dialogue #2

Mary: Now that we've looked at some market trends, let's go back to discussing your interests in these fields.

Joe: It's back to interests, huh. What about looking at the skills we have for these jobs.

Mary: Maybe you would like to run this group, Joe. You seem to have all the ideas.

Joe: I'm only trying to be logical. Interests are of pretty low importance in my book.

Dianne: I don't agree, Joe. I don't just want to jump into something because it's a job. I want to enjoy what I'm doing or I'll never last.

Mary: What do the rest of you think?

Mike, Fred, Jules, Simone—indicate agreement.

Mary: OK, let's get back to the exercise on interests.

Dialogue #2

	Member			Leader	
	Needs	Role		Approach	Skills
Joe			Used		
Dianne			Alternate		

Dialogue #3

Mary: Joe, you look like you're not really working full out on these exercises. Do your hesitations relate to our earlier discussion on interests?

Joe: Ya, I'm still not convinced and I guess I'm just the odd one out.

Mary: I didn't mean it that way. Maybe it would help if I showed you the model I'm working from...(shows model and explains).

Joe: That makes sense, I still think I have a point, but guess that I'll have to go along.

Mary: Maybe, we need to discuss as a group the way we have been relating with one another and how to make decisions in the group. (Group is brought together for a process discussion).

Dialogue #3

	Member			Leader	
	Needs	Role		Approach	Skills
Joe			Used		
			Alternate		

2.   In the above three dialogues, identify the various group processes.

Chapter 9

Working Stage

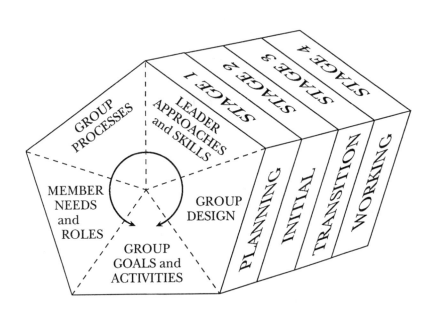

OVERVIEW

As the group moves through the Transition Stage, often an un-settled period, the members grow in self-confidence, skills and motivation. They feel much more at ease in the group and are now ready to work. This is a time of high productivity where members feel a sense of pride in their achievements and in "our" group.

During the last stage you will have built cohesion and trust and you will have brought members to a commitment to change and a readiness to take action in order to achieve their goals.

At this stage you will concentrate your efforts in the following areas:

- helping members develop specific strategies for implementing their action plans,
- encouraging and coaching them in practice or other goal achievement activities,
- encouraging further skill acquisition and refinement of goals,
- supporting them at points of uncertainty
- debriefing members after learning activities and/or skill application outside of the group,
- facilitating high levels of trust.

At the completion of this stage, members will be heavily in-volved in implementing strategies for their individual goal attain-ments. You will be preparing them for some of the sadness and loss reactions which may occur during the Termination Stage.

OBJECTIVES

As a result of reading this chapter, you will be competent to:

1. **describe the characteristics and basic theory of how a group develops in the Working Stage;**

2. describe specific group processes included in this stage;

3. describe how the group develops a high level of trust and how this contributes to a high level of group productivity;

4. explain how members' needs at this stage give rise to specific member roles which contribute to the accomplishment of group goals;

5. describe the preferred leader approaches at this stage;

6. describe the basic design principles and understand the type of structured learning activity which is recommended for the group in this stage.

CHARACTERISTICS OF THE WORKING STAGE

This is the stage where the purpose of the group starts to be fulfilled. It is called the Working Stage because members will expend a great deal of effort and energy in attempting to achieve their goals. If you want to think in more practical and physical terms: this is where people roll up their sleeves and get down to it!

Work can go ahead now because the two previous stages came first or if you like, are now past and the results of each has provided an element or condition which is vital before fruitful work can begin.

Inclusion and cohesion* were initiated from the start to provide a safe atmosphere, to remove anything that might be threatening. They are vital throughout the life of the group and have evolved, at this stage, to the point where they constitute trust. Trust continues to evolve; it is one of the absolutely essential preconditions of good work at this stage and is, therefore, a matter of major concern for you as the leader.

Members have also committed to change: had a hard look at the true nature of their difficulties and made some sort of a pact with themselves to do what they perceive is necessary to achieve

* Note: When members individually have a sense of inclusion, then all of them together experience cohesion.

their goals. This movement of the will, as we indicated in the pre- *
vious chapter, is more difficult for some people and some groups
than it is for others. It is fundamental to the work that members
do at this stage, because they understand what they must do and
why and have agreed with themselves to do it.

Both of these, trust in the group and commitment to make, *
and accomplish change, have started, in some degree, before the *
group reaches this stage. *

The group, as such, is more mature. The fact that each member has been obliged to think hard about his/her need to
change means that a good deal of self-differentiation has occurred. People are, therefore, much less worried about control. *
Another result is that they are more accepting of each other;
differences, which were previously viewed as irritants, are at least
tolerated and accepted and, in the best scenario, valued. This
change results partly also from the modeling you have done,
demonstrating understanding, acceptance and respect for the
value of each individual. As members perceive fewer threats, they
extend more trust.

Decision making is more easily accomplished and more often, *
by consensus. Communication skills are better with all the bene- *
fits one would anticipate. Members seem to feel more secure, are *
less guarded and more spontaneous. This development allows *
the group to deal more successfully with controversy and con- *
flict. Simply because members feel better, they feel more helpful *
and are more likely to take on leading (leader) responsibilities. *
Freed from concerns about control, reassured and trusting, they *
are able to involve themselves actively and to work productively. *

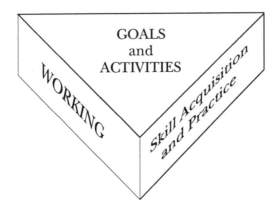

GROUP GOALS AND ACTIVITIES

The main group goals of the Working Stage centre on productivity, getting the job done. Members learn basic job search techniques, deal with unemployment issues, learn about the labour market trends or identify transferable skills in the career change process. Whatever, in fact, constitutes the principal substance of the Group or Program goals. As any manager knows, high productivity does not simply happen, there are important preconditions.

Let us take a look at the ways in which members go about working to achieve their goals. First, each member will need to examine closely and confront personal issues which may constitute blocks to employment. What members need to do is to decide upon the implications these issues hold for the actual work they must do; at this point, a very refined form of assessment.

Next, they will likely explore alternatives in order to solve their problems, an exploration which may imply adjustments: if one way is not possible, another may be used, if a strong preference simply cannot be met, a substitute may be possible. Third, the goals which are now more finely focused must be achieved and worked upon in a safe setting.

The importance of trust as a condition for work and practice—a readiness to give and receive feedback, for example—will be clear. What may not seem quite so obvious is that productivity is directly linked to a group member's ability to self-disclose. The reference here is to a process of developing and evolving self-knowledge, a self-awareness which will clarify the sense of direction: where I want to go, what I am kidding myself about, what is the real me, where may I really go and what may I really do? This is the way in which commitment to change continues in the Working Stage. Self-disclosure (we must emphasize, of the non-embarrassing sort, typical in structured learning groups) is the means of hammering out, shaping and sharpening all these ideas about themselves which permit more focused effort. It obviously derives from trust. Trust is a pre-condition for self-disclosure as self-disclosure is a pre-condition for productivity. As Corey (1982) points out:

> Individuals can decide to disclose themselves in significant and appropriate ways, or they can choose to remain hidden out of fear that if they were to reveal themselves to others they would be rejected...It is fundamental to the success of the group that honesty prevail and that a person not have to be dishonest to win acceptance. (p. 151)

Productivity is the clear group goal. At this point members are beginning to have a better idea that the group's strength and resources are greater than any of them, alone, could rally. They would be most unlikely to remark to an outsider: "I am in a group and we are working on job search skills and trust and self-disclosure and helping each other." They are aware, however, that there is a relationship between effort put into trust and self-disclosure and effort put into achieving goals.

With all this said, it is important to keep in mind that progress is rarely uninterrupted. Trust is not always perfect; self-disclosure is not invariably met with absolute sympathy. Even when conditions are optimal, members are rarely or never working on every goal. They are not doing anything which comes with easy instructions. If the work could have been done at home, they would have done it there. There will be setbacks in the attempt to achieve goals. Membership in the group will tend to help people over the rough spots, support them if they must adjust down, help them to get as far as they reasonably may and above all, make them feel good about themselves, just the way they are.

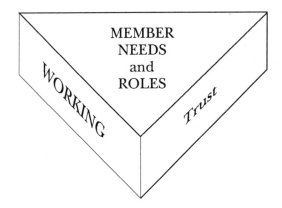

MEMBER NEEDS AND ROLES

Trust, to repeat, is important at this stage. We will briefly review the sense in which the word is being used in this book. It implies a feeling of safety. To put this another way: members feel confident that no one is going to say anything like: "Are you crazy?" or "You'll never make it!" or "I told you so!"

An important aspect of the trust we are discussing here is camaraderie, a sense of all being in the same boat. This is the kind of trust which makes it possible to open up. People in these circumstances are able to allow other people to see that they are less than perfect. What happens is a general mutual acceptance, much easier ways of relating and a sort of relaxation of defenses, permitting an easy flow of important feedback.

In this freer atmosphere the experience of helping each other enhances members' self esteem. As Johnson and Johnson (1982) state so well:

> In the maturely functioning group, all members participate and are influenced by each other according to the expertise and information each possesses. The actions of one group member truly substitute for the actions of other members as the group moves harmoniously through a division of labor toward maximizing the learning of all members. (p. 427)

This general helpfulness means that to some degree member roles become what were previously leader roles.

In the Initial Stage we assumed a kind of defensiveness in all member roles. Much of this defensiveness, as we have indicated, has diminished. People are more relaxed and helpful and member needs now cluster around goal accomplishment. Two quali- * ties flow from these facts: constructive roles predominate and, * because work is so important, roles also tend to be more * cognitive—this last arising from the now-I've-stopped-worrying-I- * can-think-much-better phenomenon with which we are all famil- * iar. As leader you will see your role, the one you have modeled, * being demonstrated by group members. As a corollary, * hindering roles are much diminished. It is still the case, however, * that group members' roles can be categorized as task, maintenance, and hindering actions. These roles, particularly characteristic of the Working Stage, are listed with the following examples.

ROLES RELATED TO TASK ACTIONS

Information and Opinion Giver

Providing facts, data and information relevant to the group's task, stating opinions, feelings or reactions to issues raised and ideas presented.

Example. "We've been talking about what employers are looking for during an interview. I have an uncle who works as a personnel officer in a large firm. I am sure he would be willing to come and talk to us about his experience. I think it might be interesting."

Initiator/Director

Suggesting objectives, activities or goals; outlining problems to be worked on, recommending procedures or a course of action for the group's work; suggesting a shift in the group's focus or method of working.

Example: "I really appreciate having this list of career options. Now I have to decide which one to follow. It would help me if we could spend some time discussing how to make a decision. Maybe we could use that grid that you showed us earlier."

Example: "I've learned a lot from doing this practice. After rehearsing, myself, and seeing the others I know what I want to do differently. If there is time I would really like to try those interviews again."

Focusing Agent

Sharpening the ideas presented; developing them; defining terminology; giving useful illustrations; building upon the ideas presented by others; looking at the consequences.

Example: "Derek (another group member) has made an interesting point. We can be whatever we want to be, but let's look at this a little closer. We all have different interests and abilities. And, also, the opportunities available to us are not the same. Don't we have to put some realistic limits on what we can achieve?"

Example: "When you say we should stop seeing ourselves as victims in the interview situation, are you saying that we ought to take the initiative?"

ROLES RELATED TO MAINTENANCE ACTIONS

Energizer

Encourages group members to work hard to achieve the group's goals.

Example. "This is fantastic. We're getting some new ideas about job search. I've really appreciated the effort everyone has put into this group."

Process Observer

Helping group members to look at their own behaviour; indicating how one sees the processes of the group and encouraging others to do so in order to better understand and improve how the group is functioning; a role adopted directly from the leader.

Example. "I think we're onto a good thing here. We've developed a whole new way of looking at this business ... Fred said one thing, Mary said a bit more and Swinder said something more. We probably couldn't have done it alone."

Compromiser

Demonstrating a willingness to reclarify ideas to arrive at consensus, to back off and to be open to altering one's own point of view.

The Compromiser has something in common with the Harmonizer, seen in the Initial stage. There is a difference because the Harmonizer is often motivated by fear (of conflict) and the Compromiser is more motivated by a desire to be helpful, and get things done, which accounts for the flexibility characteristic of this role.

Example. "Maybe you have a point, I guess there's not a whole lot we can do to create more jobs. For now, I guess we should put our dreams on hold and look at what we can do to get the jobs that are there."

Gatekeeper

Helping to keep channels of communication open; helping others to participate; facilitating the contribution they may make.

Example. "I think that Maria really made an important point in our small group discussion. She hit it on the head for me. Maria, would you tell the group why you think that there is more dignity attached to spending a paycheque than there is in earning one?"

Supporter and Praiser

Being aware of the mood, feelings and state of the group and expressing these feelings; this function may include revealing one's own feelings about the group or its members in a relative nonthreatening manner. Expresses acceptance and liking for group members.

The role of Supporter and Praiser has a clear relationship to the Energizer and the Encourager. The Supporter is less enthusiastic, perhaps, than the Energizer, but a clearly evolved form of the Encourager, applied during at the Working Stage.

Example. "I think your interviewing skills are really improving. You have a tremendous smile! It's sure to melt the heart of any interviewer!"

ROLES RELATED TO HINDERING ACTIONS

Distractor

Sharply changing the subject and directing the group away from what it is trying to work on. This may be our former acquaintance, the Grandstander, still motivated by the same need to defend him or herself, and not having made so much progress in the group as other people.

Example. (Activity-rank ordering career options). "It's hard to decide what should come first. I once knew an airline pilot who said he had visited 49 countries. That blew me away, it really did. I've only visited two countries. How about the rest of you, how many countries have you visited?"

The roles we have highlighted are not, of course, the only ones which might occur. Progress is not always in a straight line, people do slip back, feel tense and revert to earlier, more defensive (hindering) roles.

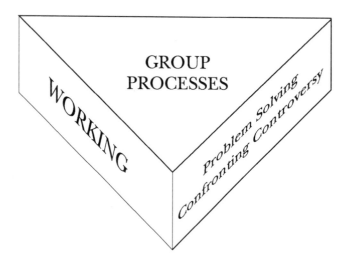

GROUP PROCESSES

As the group "changes hands" from the leader to members during the latter part of the Transition Stage, there is a tendency also for members to begin to take over handling their own processes, monitoring and making changes as required.

Four processes are important during the Working Stage of Group Development:

1. Communication.

2. Norms.

3. Decision-making.

4. Confronting the Problem.

Communication

Communication, as a result of the modeling and structured exercises you have provided, shows signs of improvement—and will continue to improve.

We have emphasized that feedback is accomplished more effectively at this stage—largely because trust is building. Another reason that feedback is easier is that judgmental labelling and insensitive invasion of privacy is minimal. Members also do listen *
better—a skill they may have learned in some of the structured *
exercises as well as from having noticed the way you listen.

In fact, your modeling may have been so successful that some *
members will have developed roles around understanding each *
other and what is happening in the group (for example, the *
Focusing Agent, Process Observer, Encourager). *

The group is now reaping the benefit of better communica- *
tion which has resulted in improved understanding and these *
benefits are noticeable in the feedback, self-disclosure and help- *
ing roles members assume. *

As leader you will continue to guide communication when necessary and to block hindering roles. Leader input is still very necessary, but, as we have said, less directive and influencing than it was.

Norms

As the group moves into its most productive stage, what changes is not so much the character of the norms as their focus. Norms * which you were obliged to make explicit, are now more implicit * and have been internalized by members. Contravening a norm, * less probable at this time, is likely to be corrected by a member rather than by you. Formerly, for example, showing concern and acceptance for each member was something you did, as leader, and members may have felt no obligation to do the same. Showing concern and acceptance is now internalized and an implicit norm. Feedback which has caused so much difficulty is now normal and hardly an occasion for comment.

What you are probably realizing is that the norms are now so * much part of the group that they are almost identical with the * Characteristics of the Working Stage. Implicit norms are: *

1. an attitude of acceptance and caring between members; *

2. risking through self-disclosure—although, obviously, the *
   risk is much smaller (because nothing bad will happen as a *
   result); *

3. feedback is now accepted as important and valuable; *

4. confrontation between members has a constructive *
   character; *

5. a clear understanding that the group is a rich resource and *
   presents an opportunity for practice. *

A new norm, that of members' commenting on processes occurring in the group, frequently emerges.

Decision-Making

The group is now more astute and skilled, perceives readily what * needs to be decided and how best to decide. Consensus is * reached with less effort and more efficiently than it was before. The general tendency is to ensure that each member's voice is heard, a practice arising from the fact that each member is now valued. Group members may do some moderating to ensure that they have input from everyone, possibly, along the following lines:

"Sonja, I know you want the group to move on, but I sense you can't see just how this decision to develop a network of contacts will affect you. I would really like to hear your concerns and I'm sure the group would, too."

As you will have gathered, consensus is now a norm.

Confronting the Problem

Some people still need to be confronted and issues need to be resolved immediately: a member feeling rejected, for example, or a decision, which is not acceptable to some members, being "railroaded". Confronting the problem as a proactive approach to creative problem resolution was discussed in the Transition Stage.

Controversies

During the Working Stage, groups often engage in controversies over substantive issues, assumptions, beliefs and ideas about what to do, why do it and how to do it. Controversies provide a positive and necessary process that leads to a finer, more precise decision. These differences of opinions and ideas occur during the time the group is trying to define, understand and solve its problems.

Everyone may agree, for example, that it is desirable to make a good impression with a resumé. The controversy may be over what type of resumé will show the job-seeker in the best light. Should it be a chronological resumé, listing all the jobs or positions the individual has held, starting at the present, of course, and working backwards, or a functional resumé, setting forth the proven skills, demonstrated abilities and so on?

There might be a heated discussion along the following lines: How can the prospective employer know you have these skills if you don't name the job where you gained them? The reply: It doesn't matter where I gained them, it only matters that I have them. Why, comes the response, would anyone take your word for it? The second person says: Why would anyone want to read a long list of places you've worked? A new voice adds that it doesn't matter as employers never read resumés but put them straight into the garbage. This remark is perhaps not ideal, but it helps to keep matters in proportion and serves also the purpose of emphasizing that the resumé should be as short as possible.

If the resumé must be short, then a solution where both functions and chronological experience are laid out is impossible. A functional resumé with dates of employment neatly and very briefly set out seems an ideal solution. But some group members want very much to emphasize the amount of experience they have had, and perhaps in this case, a chronological resumé is best.

The decision might be, as the case would seem to indicate, not that one or the other type of resumé is better. What emerges as important is to achieve a match between what the individual wishes to say about him or herself in relation to what the job being sought requires.

The process involved in handling controversies can enhance the group's effectiveness by ensuring a better quality, more creative decision—the result of having a wider variety of opinions. The fact that everyone is involved in finding the solution almost invariably means a higher level of commitment to carrying it out.

Management of the controversies in a constructive, creative way enables the group to reach the best possible solutions. The following benefits, often overlooked, result from controversy in problem solving:

1. Group members gain the broadest possible understanding of the nature of the problems and their implications by listening to the most diverse ideas and perspectives.

2. The group has more potential to arrive at a satisfactory consensus when members have been encouraged to express different opinions, beliefs, theories and ideas.

3. There is a sort of stimulation, an excitement, a positive   *
   feeling which attaches to the prospect of a new approach   *
   to a problem, a new way around an employment barrier.   *
   Hope and increased motivation are the pay-offs resulting
   from the creative interaction described in (1) and (2)
   above. "I feel good because I contributed to this new idea.
   It's a good solution and I am going to use it."

Healthy disagreement is vital to the best solution. It is often
after settling a controversy that people start saying "we" rather
than "I", when discussing issues in the group.

Helpful Leader Hints for Managing Constructive Controversy

1. Explain that controversy can be constructive and the natural
   result of members coming together with divergent values and
   opinions. Controversy is often an indicator that a range of
   more creative solutions are being sought by group members.
   Members may particularly need some reassurance if they feel
   threatened by differences of opinion.

2. Do not suppress or avoid controversy. Remember dealing with
   controversy is similar to Confronting the Problem (Chapter
   VIII). The problem is what is at issue, the personalities on
   either side are definitely not. Like problems, controversies
   should not be ignored.

3. Provide support and reassurance for members who appear
   anxious. Openly seek their opinion. Linking is a skill which
   promotes integration of ideas and is vital for resolving
   controversy.

4. Do not become more authoritarian. Resist the impulse to
   tighten your leadership and take over. Acknowledge and
   accept controversy and help members learn constructive ways
   of dealing with it.

5. Utilize active listening, clarification, and paraphrasing and, of
   course, linking as mentioned above.

6. Respond to the feelings underlying all member responses through the use of empathy, important at this stage as always.

7. Negotiate win-win solutions. Seek consensus. A solution can be found which will meet the needs of both sides, so that no member has to give in.

8. Check to see if the most creative solution, at least for this group, has been proposed. Specifically, the leader should ask, do one "go-around" to see if any improvements to the decision can be made.

Conflicts of Interest

Conflicts of interest occur when one member's interests come into conflict with another member's interests. Conflict of interest   *
is different from constructive controversy because a perfect solu-   *
tion is not necessarily possible.   *

It might be that two members have job interviews following the group meeting and both want to practice in front of you first. You only have enough time for one person to rehearse. You could have them practise at the same time or interview each other, alternating roles half way through. This solution is not perfect because neither gets as much supervision as she or he would like. But both get something and that is better than one getting nothing.

Settling and resolving conflicts of interest so that feelings stay   *
positive and the members stay committed to the group's work is   *
absolutely necessary. As the leader, you need to determine the   *
triggering events and examine the barriers to solutions. The best   *
method to use is that of mediating the conflict until both sides   *
are heard, the issues are examined and understood by both sides   *
and a creative solution is worked out and agreed to by all mem-   *
bers. Some rules for the leader to follow in mediation are: *

1. Explain that a mutually agreeable solution can be worked out.

2. Neither party is right or wrong.

3. You are not taking sides or making judgments.

4. Have each party describe the conflict. Have them stick to the content of the conflict, the problem, the difficulty. No personal remarks.

5. Then, each, in turn, explains how the conflict makes him/her feel. Being heard has a positive impact on both sides. Often this provides the impetus to seek a solution.

6. Next, each party tells how he/she would like the outcome to the conflict resolved. You want them to give you the ideal state.

7. Generate possible alternatives by brainstorming. Most likely, the conflict has a creative solution, or an alternative neither party had considered.

8. Finally, go over the agreement and get confirmation from both sides.

9. Check back later to see if this agreement is still viable, constructive, and in effect.

One final method that may facilitate the resolution of conflicts of interests is that of role reversal. Each member assumes the role of the other member and discusses the conflict from that perspective.

It must be admitted that there is not always a perfect solution to a conflict of interest situation. If two members are seeking only one job, you cannot manufacture a second. In a situation where some desirable resource or prize, obviously not within your control, is scarce, one solution is to establish a norm that people need not divulge information on this subject. They should not, in brief, be obliged to act against their own interest.

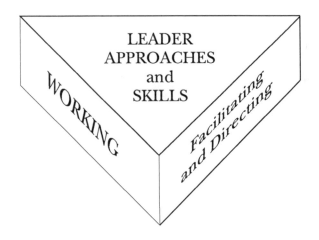

LEADER APPROACHES AND SKILLS

At this stage, you will respond as you always do, to the needs of members. Members want to work on achieving their goals and * you will ensure that they do so, facilitating practice or any other * necessary activities and serving as a resource person. *

Members will begin to assume some of your roles and some * leaders take a much less active role at this time. Your involve- * ment is as great as ever it was, even if you have a sense of being less directive. Group members have internalized a great many norms but they are not trained leaders. If you decide to inter- vene less at this time, it is because you have made this decision in the light of your knowledge and skills and not because you can- not see what use you are any more. Members may work very well but matters could go wrong and then you must intervene. It could be that members are very aware that something is amiss and call you in to settle a controversy or supply some information. It could be that only you know that things are not as they should be and then you take appropriate action.

Generally at this stage you will use a facilitating or delegating * approach. It could be, however, that the whole group starts in on * an activity wrong and you may then do some simple directing. *

You will, at this stage, monitor the group and give it cues *

(help it, facilitate the work) as necessary, arrange appropriate *
activities and encourage (a form of facilitating): remind the *
group of its achievements and urge it forward. You continue, as *
always, to model.   *
    Concrete examples of the approaches and skills that you
might use in this stage follow. As we have done in previous
chapters, these approaches and skills are set out as responses to
typical Working Stage member roles.

1. *Member Statement:*

"We've been talking about what employers are looking for during an interview. I have an uncle who works as a personnel officer in a large firm. I'm sure he would be willing to come and talk
to us about his experience. I think it might be interesting."

Role: Information and Opinion Giver.
Feeling: Involved, informed, positive.
Unspoken: "I can help this group."

Leader Response:

"You're right, we have talked a lot about the interview. It might
be helpful to get some hints from a person with your uncle's experience. What do the rest of you think about having him come
in?"

Approach: Facilitating.
Skills: Supporting, Consensus-taking.
Unspoken: "Useful suggestion, but does the group support
             this?"

2. *Member Statement:*

"Derek (another group member) has made an interesting point.
"We can be whatever we want to be,' but let's look at this a little
closer. We all have different interests and abilities, and also the
opportunities available to us are not the same. Don't we have to
put some realistic limits on what we think we can achieve?"

Role: Focusing Agent.
Feeling: Positive but cautious.
Unspoken: "I am going to try, but I'm scared I won't make it."

Leader Response:

"So you see that each of us needs to work within a realistic frame-work. We need to balance our dreams and opportunities. What do others think?"

Approach: Facilitating.
Skills: Restating, Questioning, Consensus-taking.
Unspoken: "Others must be scared too, I'd better check."

3. *Member Statement:*

"When you say we should stop seeing ourselves as victims in the interview situation, are you saying that we ought to take the initiative?"

Role: Focusing Agent.
Feeling: Positive.
Unspoken: "I want to get this straight because maybe we can get a better picture of what we might do."

Leader Response:

Note. The Focusing Agent is working this matter out with another member.

Leader: "It's really good to see how well you can think these things out without any help from me."

Approach: Delegating.
Skills: Reinforcing.
Unspoken: "They are getting the idea."

4. *Member Statement:*

"I think that Maria really made an important point in our small group discussion. She hit the nail on the head for me. Maria, would you tell the group why you think that there is more dignity attached to spending a pay cheque than there is to earning one?"

Role: Gatekeeper.
Feeling: Supportive, excited.
Unspoken: "She understands me."

Leader Response:

"Liz, Maria's comment had quite an impact on you. Maria, would you be willing to share your ideas with the rest of us?"

Approach: Facilitating.
Skills: Reflection, Questioning.
Unspoken: "Others need to hear this too."

5. *Member Statement:*

"I really appreciate having this list of career options. Now I have to decide which one to follow. It would help me if we could spend some time discussing how to make a decision. Maybe we could use the grid that you showed us earlier."

Role: Initiator/Director.
Feeling: Involved, focused.
Unspoken: "I know what I want and what we should be doing."

Leader Response:

"You would like to have some way of organizing your thinking about your options. I noticed others nodding when you were speaking. Would it be useful for everyone to spend some time looking at decision making methods?"

Approach: Facilitating
Skills: Paraphrasing, Immediacy, Consensus-taking.
Unspoken: "Good point. Others need to work on this as well."

6. *Member Statement:*

"I've learned a lot from doing this practice. After rehearsing, my-self, and seeing the others I know what I want to do differently. If there is time I would really like to try those interviews again."

Role: Initiator/Director.
Feeling: Excited, motivated.
Unspoken: "I am going to learn this well."

Leader Response:

"So the practice has been really helpful for you. John and Ed seem to see it the same way. What would everyone else think about having another round of interview practice?"

Approach: Facilitating/Delegating.
Skills: Reflection, Linking, Consensus-taking.
Unspoken: "They are really working hard to improve."

7. *Member Statement:*

"I think we're on a good task here. We've developed a whole new way of looking at this business...Fred said one thing, Maria said a bit more and Swinder said something more. We probably couldn't have done it alone."

Role: Process Observer.
Feeling: Encouraged, supportive.
Unspoken: "I feel safe and trust this group."

Leader Response:

"You're pretty happy with what has been happening today. I have also noticed that we seem to be doing some good work. Has any-one else noticed it too?"

Approach: Facilitating (mobilizing group resources).
Skills: Empathy, Immediacy, Questioning.
Unspoken: "This group is really moving now."

8. *Member Statement:*

"This is fantastic! We're getting some new ideas about job search. I've really appreciated the effort everyone has put into this group."

Role: Energizer.
Feeling: Invigorated, appreciative.
Unspoken: "I'm really making progress!"

Leader Response:

"You feel as if all of the work has been worthwhile. Everyone working together in the group has really helped you. The energy spent is really paying off."

Approach: Facilitating.
Skills: Paraphrasing, supporting.
Unspoken: "You have worked well."

9. *Member Statement:*

"I think your interviewing skills are really improving. You have a tremendous smile! It's sure to melt the heart of any interviewer!"

Role: Supporter and Praiser.
Feeling: Appreciative.
Unspoken: "I value you and your special contribution."

Leader Response:

"Tom's comments have really opened your eyes about how you come across during an interview. You're a bit surprised by the information, and really glad he let you know. Can anyone else add anything to what Tom has suggested?"

Approach: Facilitating.
Skills: Empathy, Supporting, Questioning.
Unspoken: "This honest feedback is really moving this group and it is good someone besides me is supporting it."

10. *Member Statement:*

"Maybe you have a point. I guess that there's not a whole lot that we can do to create more jobs. For now, I guess we should all put our dreams on hold and look at what we can do to get those jobs that are out there."

Role: Compromiser.
Feeling: Resigned but also motivated.
Unspoken: "I've got to get going. I need work."

Leader Response:

"You now see the importance of directing your efforts toward job search. That's what this group is really for."

Approach: Influencing.
Skills: Supporting, reflecting.
Unspoken: "I need to reinforce Jim's decision."

11. *Member Statement*

(Activity-rank ordering career options) "It's hard to decide what should come first. I once knew an airline pilot that said he had visited 49 countries. That blew me away, it really did. I've only visited two countries. How about the rest of you, what countries have you visited?"

Role: Distractor.
Feeling: Threatened.
Unspoken: "I don't want to do this."

Leader Response:

"Norm, I have noticed a couple of times when we have been going to practice interviewing that you seem to want to discuss something else. That seems to delay what we were going to do. I'm wondering if you are feeling uneasy with having to practice in front of others."

Approach: Facilitating.
Skills: Immediacy.
Unspoken: "I know how you feel, but you need to get on with it."

Practical Leader Suggestions for the Working Stage

1. Whenever possible, use linking to promote member-member rather than member-leader interactions.

2. Have group members work with each other to fine tune plans and goals before you provide your input.

3. Allow and encourage group members to give feedback to one another regarding group practice activities such as interviewing, resumé writing, etc.

4. Be prepared for possible setbacks! Some members may balk at setting goals or practising certain approaches to job search. Work with these individuals to help them figure out what is stopping them.

5. Other challenges may come when someone has reported an unsuccessful job interview. Give feedback to the individual about what to do differently another time, how to reformulate a goal, or simply point out that everything was done correctly but no job was available at this time.

6. Encourage the tendency in group members to take responsibility for running the group, i.e., making sure that activities start on time, making sure that everyone understands before moving to another activity.

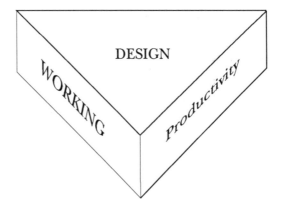

DESIGN

In order to move the group beyond the earlier stages, you need *
to design or select activities which give members the opportunity *
to work together on tasks which are personally relevant and *
which involve them with other group members. At this point you *
may become less centrally involved in the activities as group *
members depend more on one another for feedback and assis- *
tance. In other words, what members are doing now in the struc- *
tured activities would look very "high-risk", indeed, from the *
viewpoint of the Initial Stage. These activities are now possible to *
the degree that trust has been built and feedback is possible.

As leader you still have an important role as monitor and facilitator. Debriefing serves as an important focus for your efforts at
this time.

We have provided two examples of dialogues which might be
part of a learning activity at this stage and have put a heavy emphasis on the four major questions involved in the debriefing
process. Following these dialogues is a sample activity, appropriate to this stage.

Example

This is a job-search group which has just finished practising, in pairs, the job interview. The dyads have now re-formed into the large group and you will debrief.
You start with the following question:

Question 1

Leader: What did you feel like, what did you experience while you were carrying out the activity? (Because there were two people involved, it is a good idea to do an "inner" and an "outer" de-brief, the experience for the speaker and for the listener.)

Inner	*Outer*
Frank:	Daphne:
I felt very self-conscious, sort of silly. But I made myself pretend it was the real thing so I finally did get into it. I tried hard to remember everything and I think I did. It was a big effort—that was what I felt like: this is hard. But I like it!	Yeah, I thought he was going to laugh right at the beginning. But then he kind of got himself together and he sure told me everything I wanted to know.

Leader: I'd like to learn a little more about what you both feel now.

I did O.K. It isn't the sort of thing you enjoy but I thought I did well.	He struck me as a "strong candidate" as they say. I'd have hired him, I just wish he'd have smiled at me or something. He was a little, well, intense? Overwhelming?

Georgia:

Harold:

I felt excited. I've done interviews wrong lots of times and I was sure going to do it right now. I wanted to be real sure the interviewer knew I was in control of myself. This person was gonna remember me for sure.

I don't think she came over as quite as driven and determined as she sounds.

I had the feeling that she was acting like a good little girl doing her party piece. But quite likeable you know—she was a nice person.

Leader: I'd like to hear a little more about what you both feel now.

I think I did everything right. But I still don't feel very happy.

She seemed all right, but sure was tense. And it might have been better if she'd shown a little more interest in the job. Not acted quite so much as if she had it all sewn up.

Question 2

Leader: Let's see if we can make some sense out of all this, see if we can analyze what happened.

Melanie: Well, it sure seems as if they both know what to *do* in an interview, what to do first and what next. Stuff like that.

Vishnu: Like a dance routine?

Melanie: Sort of.

Leader: There seems to be a feeling that things went well but could have gone better. Let's talk to our stars. Frank and Georgia, what happened?

Georgia: Maybe it was a little like a dance routine for me— maybe I could have loosened up a little but I was trying so hard!

Angela: Listen, Georgia, you did *good*, kid. Knowing the routine is important.

Leader: Thanks, Angela, it's important Georgia knows she really did do well. Frank, what do you think?

Frank: It was pretty good practice. I was trying to work everything in and I feel that I did do that—or anyhow, I ony left out a smile or two.

Question 3

Leader: Do you think we all learned anything from this activity?

Angela: We learned we're all pretty good at this stuff now.

Leader: That's true, there's a world of difference. Is there anything new?

Carl: What it seems to me is that we all concentrate too hard on ourselves and don't think enough about what's happening with the interviewer.

Georgia: I guess that's right. I have to remember to try and get some questions ready about the job. (Laughing) Maybe like some rehearsed spontaneity.

Vishnu: Well, I think that's important, Georgia, because the employer may feel he has something really nice to offer in this job or whatever, and it may be polite—or even kind— to show you think so too!

Leader: Sounds good! Frank?

Frank: I am gonna *smile*!

Question 4

Leader: How can you apply what's happened here after you leave the group?

Vishnu: It seems what we should do: get the interview ideas down to a routine, all our qualifications and stuff.

>   Then concentrate on making the interviewer feel
>   good, you know kind of like we do for each other here.

Leader: Sounds like you've got it all sewn up. Anyone else?

Lindsay: Yeah. The next time you meet a wonderful person at a
          party, have your routine down pat then concentrate on
          making *them* feel wonderful. They'll love it! Love it!

Leader: ! ! !

Example B

This is a support group for handling job loss.

Members have been at work in small groups generating the ten top strategies for coping with job loss. The group has now been through the process of rank ordering their several contributions and have, in fact, the list before them.

It is:

1. support from family and friends
2. career counselling
3. thinking positively
4. survival jobs
5. re-training
6. volunteer work
7. financial assistance
8. pacing job search
9. networking
10. physical activity

You will now de-brief.

Question 1

Leader:	What did you feel like while you were working on this activity?
Raschid:	I felt a lot—all mixed. Often I think well, I'm not mad anymore, but then I think why am I here doing this? I used to just be thinking what I'd do on a Saturday night!
Clem:	Yeah. I felt the same. It's hard making yourself do this....
Raschid:	Because you think you shouldn't have to. Then I sort of forced myself and it got kind of interesting.
Jennifer:	Me, too. I feel mad, resentful, you know. Then I thought, I mean I *was* still mad, why should I let those jerks ruin my life? Who needs them? I can get along some way!
Maretta:	I simply don't bother getting mad anymore. I have too many other crises staring me in the face: my mother's ill and can't work, my kid—you know, the one whose got the hearing problem?—they're making an awful fuss about his hearing aid. I've just got to survive—too many people depend on me!
Clem:	I got there quick, too. We have to live so let's start thinking how we can manage.
Raschid:	Things got better when we started really working on the list. I began to feel good.
Jennifer:	Yeah, like we're fighting back. I had that kind of onward and upward feeling.
Clem:	I had a real good feeling, as if I was back at work and we were having a staff meeting deciding on a new project.
Maretta:	I never felt that good and I never was in a staff meeting—but I felt grateful we were going to do something—I mean even if it's only a little help! And

so grateful, it just means so much to have you people with me—not to feel I have to carry everything alone!

Raschid: I'm with you - especially Jennifer. I felt good to be thinking what I could *do!*

Question 2

Leader: Should we take a look at what happened? Analyze what went on?

Raschid: It's not hard! We started out feeling really down and angry and we worked our way out.

Leader: Anything else?

Jennifer: It's really more than that. We did start out feeling bad—depressed, maybe. And the activity seemed especially good, thinking of ways to cope, really to take us out of the depression. I mean the activity made sense.

Maretta: It had to! I couldn't have made myself think about the best way to plant grass!

Jennifer: The activity was good, though I liked it.

Clem: I think it is that it was good to be doing something...

Question 3

Leader: Do you think that doing this particular task helped you to look at anything in a different way? Did you learn anything particular?

Jennifer: We learned some good things to do. And I think I also learned I could be a lot worse off. When I think of the problems some people have.

Maretta: Like me, you mean? I'm used to problems! It's you people all this is so hard on!

Raschid: Well, I didn't learn that losing your job is lots of fun...but may be there are better ways of dealing with it or worse ways. Or you can do what I was doing—nothing. It's better to figure out a way, decide what you're going to do.

Question 4

Leader: Is there some way you can apply this information in everyday life?

Maretta: Not everything on the list applies to me but some of it will be useful.

Clem: It made me think: bad things do happen in life and it isn't always my fault. That was important to me. It wasn't exactly what we were supposed to be doing but I'll never say those rotten things to myself again. I was really hard on myself and it was no help.

Raschid: If something like this happens you shouldn't sit around and feel terrible. You should figure out what you're going to do!

Example of a Structure Design Activity

Following is an example of an activity which helps group members explore their interests in greater depth.

TITLE: INTERESTS—RELATIONSHIP TO LIFE STYLE

Time Required: 86 minutes

Goals

1. To capture information about abilities, personal style and general life style issues which are a part of interest.

2. To organize and clarify the information on interests.

3. To connect the information that was acquired to job preferences.

Group size

   (i) large group (ii) dyads

Materials

   paper and pencil for each member; hand-out questions to each member

Physical Setting

   (i) large room (ii) chairs

Description of Activity: Members become aware of how interests contain important information about their abilities, personal style and general life style issues.

Procedure:

1. Instruct members of the group to divide into dyads. (5 min.)

2. Explain to members:

   (a) that "A" will interview "B";

   (b) that "B" will interview "A";

      (i) to discover two (2) interests,

      (ii) using questions to produce an in-depth interview focusing on values (that is open-ended questions) rather than a great deal of superficial information (such as might be acquired by closed questions),

      (iii) "teasing out" information on abilities, personal styles and lifestyle;

   (c) "A" will use the following questions (pass out copies) and will have 15 minutes for the interview.

      (i) What are your interests?

(ii) How did they develop over time?

(iii) How do these interests relate to other aspects of your life?

(iv) Describe one occasion when the pursuit of each of these interests went particularly well and one time when it did not go well.

(v) With reference to (iv) above, what made each situation particularly positive or negative for you?

(d) at the end of 15 minutes, "A" and "B" will change roles.

3. After allowing the necessary time for both interviews, (about 30 minutes), reconvene the group in a large circle.

4. Debrief activity in large group.

(a) Ask members for information on the following:

(i) what they thought or felt about the exercise;

(ii) insights gained, (analyze and make sense), (10 min.);

(iii) how these new insights throw light on reasons for job preferences, (abstracting and generalizing), (15 min.);

(iv) the usefulness of the in-depth exploration techniques, (applying what was learned), (15 min.

5. Summarize (2 min.).

POINTS TO REMEMBER

The Working Stage of Group Development is where the work of the group gets done, where the purpose is fulfilled. During this stage, members learn new skills and practice them. This stage requires the bulk of time in the program. Time and attention need to be paid to carrying out the required activities so as to enhance each member's chance of being successful.

The following points have been emphasized as important in this chapter:

- **The leader needs to:**

  1. **continue to build trust within the group,**

  2. **ensure that the group is productive by designing activities which will produce the needed skills, and,**

  3. **provide adequate maintenance by making sure that the group processes are functioning for optimum benefit.**

- **Members' goals involve:**

  1. **examining and confronting personal barriers to unemployment,**

  2. **learning new skills,**

  3. **practising these skills.**

- **Group processes are communication, internalization of norms, decision making, and confronting the problem especially as this applies to controversy and conflicts of interest.**

- **The leadership approach is to delegate, facilitate and to act as a resource to the members. Leadership skills include primary accurate empathy, information giving, linking, supporting, clarifying, paraphrasing, consensus-taking, questioning, process-observing, goal-setting and contracting.**

The group feels proud, energized and committed to work during this stage. New learnings, skills, and renewed commitment to career change or job hunt signal successful conclusion of the Working Stage.

POINTS TO PONDER

1. How would you feel, as the leader, about relinquishing some of your directing and influencing activities at this stage?
2. What do you think might happen in your group if, at this stage, some members left because they found jobs?

EXERCISES

1. Comment on the following dialogue in terms of member needs and roles and leader skills. Suggest alternate leader functions and skills where appropriate. As before, these exercises are just for practice.

Characters: **Leader:** Gerry
Group members: Lorraine, Marv, Chris, Darcy, Jeannette and Miranda.

Dialogue

Marv: A major problem or barrier for me is my lack of education. But, you know, I really don't see any way around it. I just can't see myself sitting in a classroom for any longer than a year or two.

Jeanette: Maybe you don't have to, Marv. I've heard of colleges where if you pass the entrance exam, you're in. You don't have to waste your time on upgrading.

Darcy: I wouldn't be quite so quick to downgrade upgrading, Jeannette. I've taken a few courses and they really helped me.

Leader: Upgrading is important, not only for developing background skills, but also for confidence building. It can be a real help.

Miranda: I think we might be getting a little off track here talking about upgrading. What do you think, Marv?

Marv: Ya, I'm not that concerned about what courses I'm taking, for me it's how long I have to go to school.

Leader: Thanks for getting us back on track, Miranda, let's see if we can be clearer about Marv's concern.

Chris: I think that, as a start, what I would like Marv to describe are his goals. If I can understand where Marv wants to end up, then certain things need to be done.

Leader: That sounds like a good idea. Marv, would you mind briefly stating the goals you are starting from?

Marv: Well, I guess I'm like everyone else, I want to have a good job with a decent wage. I'm interested in working with people and thought that I wouldn't mind being a counsellor, or something.

Chris: There's a lot of different types of counsellors. Did you have something specific in mind?

Marv: Well, I was thinking of being a counsellor in a half-way house. I think that I can relate to people trying to get their act together.

Leader: You talked earlier, Marv, about your experience in a half-way house. I wonder if it would be helpful for you to talk with some of the counsellors working there and see what they have in terms of education.

Miranda: I can also give you the name of a fellow that I know who is working in a half-way house.

Marv: That sounds like a good idea. I will get that name from you, Miranda, and call a few of the counsellors tonight.

	Member			Member	
	Needs	Role		Approach	Skills
Jeannette			Used		
Darcy			Alternate		
Miranda					

2. In reviewing the above dialogue, indicate evidence of high levels of trust and productivity.

3. Describe the group procedures included in the above dialogue.

4. What are two design principles which apply particularly to this stage?

Chapter 10

Termination Stage

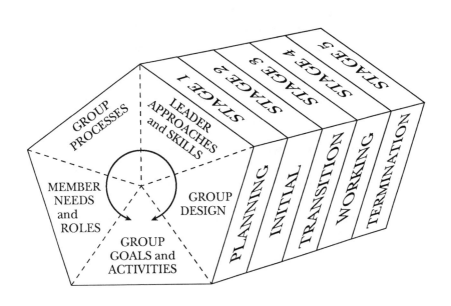

OVERVIEW

During the Working Stage, group members have developed into a mature, hardworking, productive group, learning how to get along, help each other and, altogether, they have become a cohesive, trusting unit. Then, as it begins, the group has to end. No matter how hard the group prepares for and understands the process of termination, members still find this reality to be abrupt and emotional, filled with sadness and excitement, anticipation and fear.

Even though the Termination Stage signals the end of the group's work, essential goals still need to be achieved. Too often groups "just end" without focusing carefully on what has been learned or determining specific ways to apply these learnings in the absence of ongoing group support. You don't want to leave members wondering: "So what was all that about?" Too often groups end without dealing with the sadness at parting. Relationships which have turned out to be extremely important will need to be adjusted and ways and means for developing post group support and resources, set in place.

During the Working Stage you will have ensured that members were involved in implementing strategies for their individual goal attainment. You will have started to prepare them for the sadness and loss reactions which will probably occur during the Termination Stage.

At this stage, you will concentrate your effort in the following areas:

- ensuring the integration of knowledge and skill learning;

- preparing group members for the transfer of knowledge and skills;

- assisting the development of individual contracts for future goals;

- ensuring that members say "Good bye".

OBJECTIVES

As a result of reading this chapter the reader will be competent to:

1. **describe the characteristics of the Termination Stage of Group Development;**
2. **describe the important goals which face the group at this stage;**
3. **describe the specific group proccsses of the Termination Stage;**
4. **identify member roles which emerge at the end of the group;**
5. **describe the leader skills and approaches most suited for assisting members to deal with termination of the group:**
6. **explain how specific activities are needed to accommodate member needs which arise around the realities of leaving the group.**

CHARACTERISTICS OF THE TERMINATION STAGE

The leader has striven over the past three stages to assist and guide the group to become highly productive and accomplish goals. Productivity required the establishment of working relationships high in trust. Very frequently members have enjoyed high levels of output and considerable personal satisfaction in the group. The learning, trust, acceptance and support which members have managed to achieve means that the ending of a group is an important stage possessing unique characteristics.

The members often appear subdued and sad at the thoughts of the ending of this meaningful experience. They tend to engage in behaviours which might be described as avoidant: they may pull back, may not participate, may stay away and stall for time and generally goof off. They may also request extra sessions. These types of behaviour indicate pretty clearly that members are reluctant to accept the idea that the group is over. This reluctance occurs in direct relation to the degree to which the group has been highly productive and has provided a sense of meaning, some structure and a source of community support. You wil hope that members will experience excitement about the possibilities awaiting them when they leave the group—and so they do—but many will also feel anxious at the prospect of facing the world solo again.

On a more specific level, the leader will notice several of the following things happening in the Termination Stage.

- The group processes can shift significantly away from a smooth-   *
ly functioning and productive, interdependence to a pattern   *
similar to that seen earlier where members seek more direction   *
from you. Seeking-out direction will most often take the form   *
of requesting support in refining an action plan, help in selecting the best type of follow-up training program, etc.

- For many members, the end of the group is a time to discuss   *
and review their accomplishments and the good times they   *
have had together. The nature of these reflections is obviously   *
influenced by the degree to which the group program has
been able to satisfy the goals for which it was established and
the level of individual member satisfaction.

- Members can often be observed making arrangements to con-   *
tinue contacts and friendships into the post-group period,   *
most often for support or as a continued resource link.

- A group which has enjoyed success in achieving its goals often   *
plays "Do you remember?", recollecting critical points in the   *
life of the group. Often, this type of reminiscing helps mem-   *
bers bring closure to the life of the group as they have come to
know it. Statements of where they are going next in their career paths assist in the business of saying "Goodbye" and parting from the group.

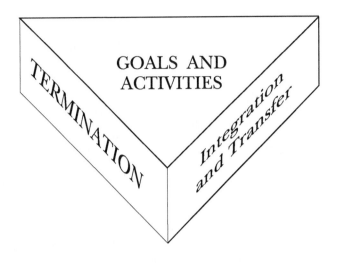

GROUP GOALS AND ACTIVITIES

Three major goals still face the group in the Termination Stage. First, members need to *integrate* what they have learned during the program. Integration of knowledge refers to an understanding of the way everything members have learned fits together.

Let us suppose that members have been in a career choice group. They will have identified, for example, useful working experience (and, maybe, life experience, too), skills, aptitudes and interests and, perhaps, the local labour market. The integration is a perception of how these elements affect one another, a recognition of the way and experience enhances a skill, and provides a better understanding of self, and, often contributes greatly to a sense of self-worth. This awareness, now well-integrated, serves as a jumping-off point for further action (job search, training and so on). Integration will make possible but not, of course, guarantee transfer (the second goal) of new knowledge and skills to the process of goal achievement after the group ends.

You will recall a very similar step occurs in Individual Counselling where skills learned are viewed in the light of how they may be tranferred to other life situations.

What have I learned.

What skills do I have now, that I didn't have before?

Are my goals the same now as when I began?

If not, what changes have I made?

What do I still have to do to achieve my goals?

These questions obviously form part and substance of the reflective need which is so characteristic of this stage. The answers provide each member with realistic and convincing signs of progress and productivity.

The new skills are not the only pluses members will take with them. From the experience in the group, members often derive a new sense of confidence and enthusiasm. "Integration" refers not just to what has been learned, it includes also what has been experienced.

Members should also clarify, review, and evaluate the ways in which the group experience has affected them. If they are able to interpret and summarize what their experience has been, they are well on the way toward assimilating and integrating it. From this perspective, members need to deal with several questions:

a) What did this experience tell me about myself, that I didn't know before?

b) Did I enjoy the relationship with other members?

c) Did this relationship make me feel good about myself?

d) What do I most want to remember about the group and the other members?

Evidence of skill and knowledge gains functions as a sort of motor, propelling members to the second major activity of the *Termination Stage: setting new goals.* Members need to identify their future goals (if, by chance, they have not done so by this point). As a corollary, they must necessarily identify which of the newly-acquired skills they will probably need.

Each member needs to be encouraged to make a new commitment for continued change once the group has finished.

A behavioural contract is one way to ensure this change takes place. Stated simply, the "behavioural contract" is a statement which the member develops as a result of his or her learning in the group. This statement describes several specific actions that the member plans to carry out, and describes how actions are to be done. Frequently a contract or statement such as this, reviewed with the other members and the leader of the group, helps members to stay committed to acting on their goals. This plan serves the purpose of transferring and generalizing the learning from the group experience to the members' everyday life situations.

All this said, the third major activity for members is to end * *relationships* and deal with all the separation issues of loss and * sadness. The major separation issue, for those who retain clear * memories of the tension and sadness they experienced before joining the group, is fear of being without the support and challenges that the group provided.

Members need to recognize the achievements of both the group's and their own hardwork. It's a time for a pat on the back. This recognition acts as the summarizer and integrator of the group's life and signals the finish of the work. It frees the group members to part company.

It is also necessary to evaluate the quality of your leadership, a process which starts by eliciting member feedback. From this information it is possible for group members and you to deduce what was good and what must be changed—and sometimes, how. This evaluation provides information which is also important for accountability—and which may result in improvements "next time": more refined guidelines for selection, a better design, more carefully worded publicity, etc., described in more detail in the next chapter.

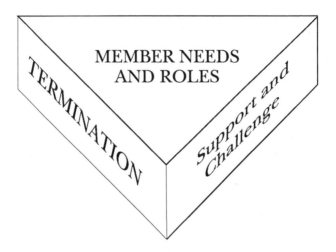

MEMBER NEEDS AND ROLES

As members conclude their participation in a productive group they are usually feeling positive about the time spent and what they have achieved. The recent follow-up study of job search groups by Amundson and Borgen (1986) indicates that group members regard their involvement in the job search group as the highlight of their unemployment experience. (Although, admittedly, on a life–time scale, it might rate a little lower!) The positive sense of renewed purpose and increased self-esteem lasts for a considerable length of time and, as you will recall, seems to exist whether or not an individual member finds work.

The feelings of loss and the reactions associated with the Termination Stage may find members in one of Kubler-Ross's (1969) stages of grieving.

Denial

Some members will act as if nothing is going to change and walk   *
out of the door at the last session as if the group were going to   *
meet again as usual.   *

Anger

Some members will show anger toward the leader and other   *
group members as a result of the anticipated loss of support   *

and/or feelings of being overwhelmed at having to undertake *
job search on their own. They may also resort to passive aggres- *
sion where, for instance, they will avoid completing assignments *
or come to the group late.   *

Bargaining

Some will try to extend the group (with the leader) and have *
additional meetings.   *

Depression

Some will feel depressed about the group ending. Members will *
be confused and anxious and feel very unsure about whether
they can carry on without the support and encouragement from
group members. They may feel overwhelmed.

Acceptance

Some will see their time in the group as a positive experience *
and will be sorry to see it end, but they will, also, feel stronger *
and ready to meet the challenges that lie ahead.

As members come to terms with the end of the group, the hope
is that they will move toward Acceptance. The other hope is that
they will be able to continue using the newly acquired skills without the support of an ongoing group.

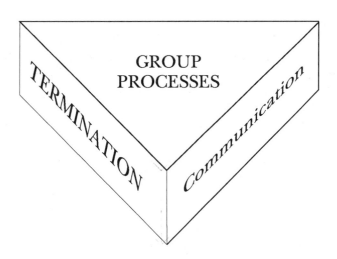

GROUP PROCESSES

Communication

The single most important group process of this stage is that of *
communication. If the leader does not handle communication *
properly, members may leave with unresolved issues and feelings. Then members may discount the group's impact. Because
of the increase in emotions—sadness, excitement, anticipation
and fear during this stage—you need to communicate with em- *
pathy and clarity but still challenge members through immediacy *
and confrontation.   *

Keeping in focus the sense of loss that will be expressed
behaviourally by some members, the leader must be prepared to
intervene immediately. "Mike, you said the group helped a little.
Your voice sounds sad. I wonder if you are scared and a little
overwhelmed to think you will be carrying out all these actions
on your own. I am wondering how many of the rest of the group
feel the same way?" The leader must help members confront
their sadness. But they must also be encouraged to acknowledge
their strengths. "Al, you talk about missing the friendship of the
members and finding new friends and how uncertain that makes
you. How about some feedback for Al on how he contributed to
the group?" With luck, someone will say something like: "Well,
Al, you were the one who always recognized how we felt inside.
That made me feel good."

Summarizing the experiences and learnings of the group,
assists individuals in the transfer of the skills to everyday life.

The use of communication skills in contracting for continued
work on goals is a significant part of what occurs during this
stage. Again, through effective planning, the leader guides the
individual members to initiate and develop contracts that will enable them to achieve their goals. A leader might say, "Your contract would be more effective and you would be able to measure
the success of your goal better if you wrote the objectives more
specifically. For example, you could state: 'I plan to complete
three job interviews in the first two weeks following this program'
rather than saying you intend to set up some job interviews. It
isn't easy to be specific. I am sure others are having the same
difficulty. Let's do your first goal on the board."

Norms

A norm of the Working Stage which is still important is contin- *
ued effort towards the achievement of whatever are the Group or *
Program Goals. *
These norms are reinforced by means of contracting, direction giving, etc. For example, if members work on a plan for continued job search or future career exploration, the group norm
of working toward high achievement is maintained.
Another important norm is reaffirmed during this stage, that *
of confidentiality. You will help the group deal with ways to *
maintain confidentiality as members talk about the group
experience with others outside the group. Talking about what
occurred in the group in a general way is fine, but members
should be sensitive to what was personal. It may happen that
George, for example, in his comfort and trust in the group,
disclosed negative feelings about the reluctance of one of the
employment counsellors to help him. Certainly, if these
comments were discussed outside the group and heard by the
counsellor, both George and the counsellor could be affected in
a negative way.

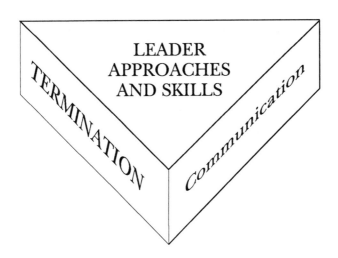

LEADER APPROACHES AND SKILLS

A skillful leader confronts and guides the members in a discovery *
of satisfactory ways to close relationships. At least a part of this *
task can be done by paying attention to setting goals which *
members work toward once the group has finished. By doing *
this, the attention of members becomes focused to the future
rather than centering on existing connections.

Modeling is a particularly important leader function at this
stage. The group's success in terminating is related, at least in
part, to the type of tone you can set and how you recognize and
express your own feelings around parting.

The following grid is helpful in understanding the skills you
will need to assist group members to leave the group with a sense
of completion and motivation to achieve further goals. In the
grid, the issues of loss and preparation for action (launch) which
the leader needs to deal with, are highlighted. Leader skills are *
also categorized into those that promote task actions on the part *
of the group and those that facilitate maintenance actions by *
members. Listed within the grid are the skills required by the *
leader in supporting and challenging the group as it ends.

Issues for the Leader in the Termination Stage

Loss	*Launch*
	Task
Summarizing – accomplishments of individuals and the group; (to include feedback from the leader and other members).	*Clarification* – of action plans.
	Goal Setting – refining action plans.
	Contracting – for implementation of action plans.
Integration – of learning in the group.	*Consensus* – about the best ways to face day to day realities.
Linking – different members' reactions to the group's ending.	

Maintenance

Immediacy – regarding members' reactions to the group ending.

Information giving – about how to maintain a support network in meeting needs for community, meaning and structure.

Advanced Empathy –in showing understanding of members' experience of loss.

plans.

Supporting – members to recognize what they have achieved and encouraging them to follow through on their action

Expressing confidence that members will reach their goals.

Self Disclosure – regarding leader's own reaction to group ending.

Modeling – by the leader, ways that people move into the future,taking with them specific learnings from the past.

Confronting – members who are avoiding or resisting the issue of termination or contracting.

Looking at the leader approaches implied by the skills identified in the grid, it is obvious that you will act differently from the way you did in the Working Stage, and more as you did in the Initial Stage. In the Termination Stage the leader guides *
interaction, and directly supports and encourages members. In *
other words, you will provide more direction for the members because they may be feeling confused as the group ends. As an example, the leader guides individuals to identify the strengths and plans that they can bring into action when they are functioning on their own.

Some Helpful Leader Hints

1. Acknowledge (occasionally, you may even have to stress) that the group is really ending.

2. Encourage members to express their real feelings related to loss. If members are encouraged to express their genuine feelings about having to leave the group, there will be a great deal less acting out around feelings of resistance.

3. The members want, and need to know that their group fulfilled its purpose and had its own special meaning for each of them. This need must be addressed and the purpose and meaning should be expressed. (Integration)

4. Help members review changes and reinforce these changes through goal setting and contracting for follow through.

5. Members need to tie up loose ends and finish business with the group. Some may want to say "thanks" to the other members. Others have different things they want to say. For example, Christie feels the need to explain her behaviour by saying: "I feel that I did not talk about myself as much as I wanted to and now I feel badly. Next time I am going to do that early."

6. Identify resources and key contacts outside the group which will be useful in furthering the members' goals.

7. Make plans for follow-up sessions, both individual and group.

8. Help members to evaluate their own level of goal achievement.

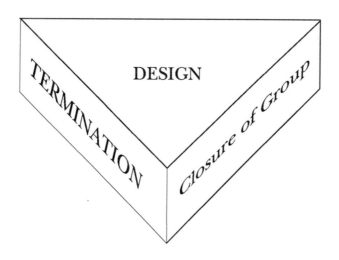

DESIGN

For this stage, you will need to design activities which give *
members an opportunity to consolidate their learning in this *
group and set a focus towards gaining a job. Secondly, you will *
need also to assist members in ending their relationships with *
the other members in a satisfying fashion. *

Example of a Structured Design Activity

What Now? This activity is designed to help members consider
ways in which the group has helped them to meet their needs for
community, meaning, and structure (Toffler, 1980), and to plan
ways for them to meet these needs when the group has ended.

TITLE: WHAT NOW?

Time Required: 2 hours

Goals/Objectives

a) To identify ways in which members meet needs for
    community, meaning and structure.

b) To have members share information with the rest of the group (whole group).

c) To find areas of commonality and difference in members' approaches to need fulfillment.

d) To develop concrete plans for future need fulfillment.

Group Size: Large group

Materials: Index cards

Physical setting: Large room

Description of Activity:

This activity is designed to help members consider ways in which the group has helped them meet their needs for a sense of community, purpose and life structure.

Procedure:

1. Assign members into small groups of four(4).

2. Provide instructions as follows:

   a) We have spent some time talking about how work can help us meet our needs for friends (community), purpose (meaning) and how it helps us fill in our time (structure). We have also recognized that it is important to meet these needs during unemployment. What I would like us to do now is to focus on ways that you have been meeting these needs while attending the group. Please do that now. Make sure everyone has a turn. (Pass out paper/pencil.)

   b) One member is to record the key points of every person in your group. (Allow 15 minutes.)

   c) Now: consider ways that you can meet the same needs when we have finished here.

    d) Again, be sure to record the key points of every person in your group (allow 15 minutes).

3. Reconvene the group and invite members to share plans.

4. Lead a discussion to link members' statements to plans that they have for the fulfillment of these needs in the future.

5. Debrief activity.

    a) Ask members to describe their experience in this activity.

    b) "Go around" the group and complete the following stems:

        (i) I became aware...

        (ii) I learned...

        (iii) I was surprised...

6. Summarize the activity for the following:

    a) Areas of commonality.

    b) Areas of differences.

POINTS TO REMEMBER

- **In this stage, members face loss reactions as the group comes to an end.**

- **At this point members are integrating their learning and making concrete plans for the future. You need to assist with this process by incorporating structured termination activities.**

- **Typically, as the group ends members are energized and confident. They have a better sense of their capabilities and interests, more knowledge and skills regarding ways to meet their needs, and more confidence that they can cope successfully with the stresses of unemployment (although this confidence may be moderated by some uncertainty about managing on their own).**

- **Leader approaches at this stage are, as they were in the Initial Stage, to facilitate and direct. This stage requires the use of the entire range of leader skills: skills to demonstrate empathy, skills to challenge and skills to consolidate action plans.**

POINTS TO PONDER

Are there any circumstances under which you can see yourself extending a group beyond the agreed upon time limits? How much flexibility do you see yourself having in this regard?

Have you found yourself at some time in a group that just "ended" without any attempt at summarizing what was accomplished and setting future direction? What thoughts and feelings did you have about this experience?

EXERCISES

1. Comment on the following dialogue in terms of member needs and roles and leader approaches and skills. Suggest alternate leader approaches and skills and write a new leader dialogue where appropriate.

Setting: Career Exploration Group for Women Returning to Work—last of ten sessions, beginning of termination session

People: **Leader**: Grace
        Group Members: Andrea, Kathy, Ellie, Mary, Lisa, Bonita, Francis

Dialogue #1

Grace :   Well, this is our last session together and we have a full
(leader)   session today. I can't believe you have come as far as
           you have! I think you've really accomplished a lot. Now
           for our first task. You mentioned last session that you
           would like to review the grids you completed for
           evaluating your various plans.

Mary: Before we begin, Francis couldn't make it today and told me to say goodbye to everyone.

Grace: We'll miss her, it's too bad she couldn't come.

Dialogue #1

	Member			Leader	
	Needs	Role		Approach	Skills
Mary			Used		
			Alternate		

Dialogue #2

Lisa: I really feel strong today, it's good to have some solid plans and to feel that I can actually do something about them.

Bonita: That goes for me too. When I first started this group I felt so unsure of myself. You know, I'm going to miss you all.

moment of silence

Grace: As I said earlier you all accomplished so much. You
(leader) have identified your strengths and interests and now with your plans you are ready to begin job search.

Andrea: I just hope that I can do it. Having plans is one thing, putting them into action isn't going to be easy.

Kathy: I'm excited about looking for a job, but I must admit that I wish that we were all staying together for just a little while longer.

All members:
          Yeah, That would be nice, etc...

Grace: I wish that we could continue too, but it's not really
(leader) possible. I start the next group on Monday. I'll remember you though, your courage and your hopes. I've enjoyed working with every one of you.

Dialogue #2

	Member			Leader	
	Needs	Role		Approach	Skills
Lisa			Used		
Bonita			Alternate		
Andrea					
Kathy					

Dialogue #3

Grace: Well, I guess that's about all our time for today. What
(leader) do I mean 'today'? I guess that's all our time.

Andrea: Could we just review one more time the decision making steps? I know they'll really help with everything that's ahead.

Mary, Kathy: Yeah

Grace: I guess I could stay another half hour.
(leader)

Ellie: I have to go now, my kids will be waiting for me. Good-
            bye everyone.

Bonita: Yeah, I should get going too, see ya.

Lisa: Why are some of you looking so down. This isn't the
            end of the world. We'll see each other again. Let's go
            out with a smile.

Dialogue #3

	Member			Leader	
	Needs	Role		Approach	Skills
Lisa			Used		
Bonita			Alternate		
Andrea					
Ellie					

2. In the above three dialogues identify the places where the
   leader and members identify the need for concrete plans and
   the places where they recognize their loss.

3. Comment on the processes and dynamics evident in the
   above dialogues.

4. Can you think of an activity which would assist members to
   adjust to the end of the group? Describe.

Chapter 11

Post Group Stage

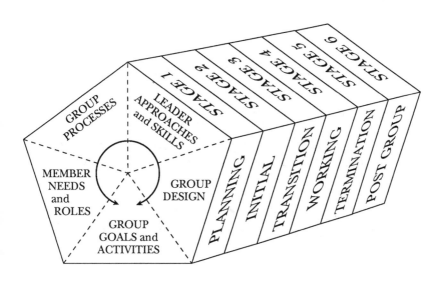

OVERVIEW

The group has been finished for some weeks and now you plan and carry out some sort of follow-up.

During the Post Group Stage the group concludes its ongoing contact. The following three main areas become the focal points for this stage: follow-up; coordination and consultation on behalf of group members; and the formal evaluation of both the group leadership and program for accountability and future group planning.

Essentially, this stage is concerned with:

• follow-up with clients

• reporting back to supervisor and colleagues

OBJECTIVES

As a result of reading this chapter the reader will be competent to:

1. **develop a plan for follow-up;**

2. **describe and understand the consultation and coordination activities that must be used to ensure success of the members and success of the program;**

3. **describe the ways in which the evaluation at this stage supplements the evaluation conducted in the Termination Stage.**

FOLLOW-UP

Follow-up serves many valuable functions for members as well as the leader. Follow-up can be broken down into three major areas:

• post-group session,

• individual follow-up by the leader with each member,

- follow-up by members with other members, individually or in small groups for support and further skill development.

Let's look at each in more detail.

Post Group Session

One effective way in which the leader can follow up group members is to conduct a post-group session after 3-6 weeks. The post-group session brings members together to evaluate the group's experience and to share in each other's successes. It can be extremely valuable because it motivates members to renewed commitment (and responsibility) for change. For those who have not found work it provides support and group resources for continued efforts. The members establish and share network contacts and build their own support structure by linking with other group members. After a post-group session, members will often be motivated to work with each other to review and practice skills.

For the leader, the post-group session is the single most effective way of evaluating the success of the group, seeing if the goals were achieved and if the program fulfilled its purpose.

Follow-up Interview

An alternative to the post-group session, and certainly one which can give a big boost to continued member effectiveness, is the individual interview. It can provide an opportunity for the following:

1. individual members can discuss the group experience and assess the degree to which their expectations were addressed;

2. you may assist members in evaluating and revising their contracts, i.e., after testing out their plans of action in the field, the members may need to modify *what* (the goals) they had set out to do and *how* (the contract) they do it;

3. you can reinforce signs of change and encourage

members' commitment to taking responsibility for their   *
own goal attainment;   *

4. you can determine the current specific needs of members   *
and assist them with an additional referral, extra resources,
other options, support, etc., as seems indicated or
necessary.

The follow-up interview should be structured. To accomplish
this, you may have each member answer the same questions or
fill out a post-group questionnaire. This information is then in
suitable shape for accountability relative to the program's
effectiveness.

The follow-up can be done by telephone if it is impossible to
arrange either a post-group session or an individual follow-up
interview. Even a short call can be encouraging for the client and
informative for the group leader. A structured interview by telephone can also still provide essential information for evaluative
purposes.

Just as the group sessions are ideally preceded by individual
interviews so they may also be followed by individual interviews.
As we have already mentioned, the informal follow-up interview
is not un-structured. You begin by citing the contract, if one was
signed, and checking that it still represents the client's goals, or
in general, making certain that the client still wants to head in
the same direction. If this is the case, you may enquire about the
extent to which the client has been able to meet the goals. The
process might conclude with referral to other resources or a
decision to supplement the group experience with individual
counselling.

In the event that the contract no longer serves its purpose,
some sort of re-evaluation may be necessary. The unserviceable
contract may require only minor changes. There will probably
not be an indication that counselling should start all over
again—although there is always that possibility.

Often re-evaluation results in the contract being re-written
more realistically in terms of what the client perceives, in the
light of experience, as more possible or more useful. When this
change in the contract is needed, it is very important that you

ensure that the client perceives the change as necessitated by a lack in the contract *not* in him or herself. The situation is treated in exactly the same way when there is no contract, only stated goals. Above all, you want to avoid having the client start worrying about his/her personal deficiencies.

Member–Member Follow-up

When the group finishes, it is important to suggest that members   * *can* follow-up on each other and stay in touch to provide support   * and/or to provide a chance to practice skills. This type of follow-   * up often is the most productive for member growth. Real friendships can develop and the ongoing support can be extremely valuable.

COORDINATION AND CONSULTATION

Coordination is a facilitative process in which the group leader   * acts on behalf of individual members to arrange resources and   * contacts, and to help ensure that members' needs and contractu-   * al commitments can be fulfilled.   *

These activities, if they are undertaken by you, must be carried out with due regard for confidentiality. You might, for example, at the client's request or with his or her concurrence, set up an appointment with another agency. *You should always obtain the client's permission to make the referral or to divulge information when you telephone; written permission is necessary for a written report. Speaking without accurate knowledge of Commission policy, as we clearly do, we strongly recommend that you seek proper authorization before contacting or dealing with outside agencies.* We would like to remind you also of the previous discussion of client confidentiality in Chapter 4. Generally, it is better if the client makes the call. In fact, many agencies will not accept appointments made on behalf of clients by second parties. The reason is that the motivation is often the caller's rather than the client's. Recourse to the help of another agency is certainly something you may recommend or discuss with a client. If you wish to be very helpful you might write the name and telephone number of the agency on a slip of paper. All the other steps are much better taken by the client.

You may, of course, make any arrangements for the use of CEIC resources when these activities are properly part of normal duties.

You may also offer an in-depth consultation to individual *
members after the follow-up interview if this service is required. *
Sometimes, individual members need additional time because of *
personal issues that have developed and you may be the best con- *
tact in a crisis situation. *

At present, no guidelines concerning either confidentiality or accountability have been established within the Commission and some uncertainty, therefore, exists around these subjects. Both these matters should, therefore, be approached with sensitivity and a due concern for law and privacy legislation. As you know, a counsellor must report to the manager, concerning a client, the goals the client selected, the barriers to employment which existed, and the progress made. These guidelines have been established in terms of individual counselling. No guidelines exist at this time on the subject of group counselling. One might assume that a client-by-client report to the manager along the same lines as the ones required for individual counselling may be introduced. *We must emphasize, however, that as authors of this book only, we cannot presume to speak for the CEIC on this matter.* The Commission will certainly develop a directive around these subjects. At present, members of CGCA or any other professional associations may follow the codes that these bodies set forth and others may certainly choose to do so.

A way around all these difficulties is to write a formal report *
for general circulation. The report should include all the usual *
details: size, purpose, target, population and so on. (An outline *
is included in the next section.) The report has the advantage of showing your manager that you have a professional approach to your job. It also leaves colleagues with the impression that you "got back" to them without anyone having lost their professional perspective.

EVALUATION

Evaluation of the group began during the Termination Stage through a structured group assessment activity. You will recall that this evaluation served two purposes; first, to assess the impact of the group experience on the members and, second, to assess the leadership of the group.

During the Post-Group Stage, you may obtain additional data through the follow-up procedures. The information from both these evaluations can be pulled together and a brief report may be written. This report is for purposes of accountability and information sharing with colleagues and supervisory staff, as we have just described. The report should focus on the following information:

(a) type of group: member needs—short and long term goals;

(b) CEIC support for the group: number of meetings, leadership of the group;

(c) evaluation results:

- goals realized (cost effectiveness if possible),

- effectiveness of leadership,

- value of various program activities,

- a few client remarks;

(d) recommendations.

This report then becomes the working paper for input from both the CEC manager and your CEC peers. With combined input and consultation among the CEC Branch personnel, a commitment, with modifications, to the original design can be made for future group employment counselling. This thorough evaluation helps formulate understanding of leadership issues and optimal ways to meet members' employment counselling needs in a group situation.

Helpful Leader Hints

1. Build in time for follow-up! Follow-up is often the first thing to be neglected but it very often holds the key to being able to determine and assist members in integrating what they have learned in the group or in the outside world of work.

2. It is possible you will have to make an effort to contact clients after the group terminates. If the member is discouraged he/she may not seek you out.

3. Prepare your report on the group and make sure that it gets circulated and discussed. Such reporting of outcomes of the program serves to inform workmates and supervisors about the work you are doing with your groups and it keeps you in the public eye.

4. Evaluate your own leadership and its effectiveness in preparation for the next group counselling program:

    (a) Meet with members (post-group) to learn about what you have done or not done to promote learning and skill development in the group.

    (b) Ask members at this point, which of the activities you presented seemed useful in finding a job and which did not.

    (c) Summarize the information gathered.

Post-group activities, then, bring closure to the life of the group. For you, having led your group through the developmental stages to maturity is no small task. You will feel a good deal of pride in the accomplishments of your group.

POINTS TO REMEMBER

- A follow-up plan for a group, should include one of the following:

    (a) post group session,

    (b) follow-up interview,

    (c) follow-up phone interview.

- Consultation and coordination on behalf of your client can assist them to meet their employment needs.

- Evaluate your program: the goals, effectiveness, and your leadership for program improvements.

- Communicate with colleagues and the manager regarding your program outcomes.

- Leader at this point adopts an eclectic attitude toward approaches and skills to be used, depending upon whether the Post-Group contact is individual or group. Or whether the leader is consulting with colleagues or supervisors with regard to evaluation.

POINTS TO PONDER

In your CEC setting, what would be the most challenging and difficult aspects of running a post group session or continuing to work with group members on an individual basis?

How will you feel about reporting the effectiveness of your group to your colleagues or to your manager?

EXERCISES

Think about your own situation and the organizational framework in which you operate:

1. What types of follow-up would be most appropriate? Are there any roadblocks you foresee?

2. Who are the people you think it important to consult?

3. What evaluation procedures would have the most impact?
    On your manager? On your colleagues? On your own
    development as a group leader?

Chapter 12

The End Launches
The Beginning

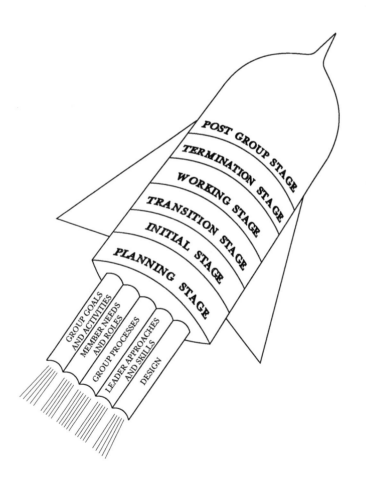

A peculiar title for the last chapter of a book! What it really signifies is:

The End:

This chapter brings to an end this book which contains the knowledge base you need for understanding group development, theory, leadership and the elements of design in groups. This point also marks the end of the text material we would like you to cover before entering the training phase.

Preparation for the Launch:

The preparation is the up-coming training workshop where you will learn to translate your knowledge into practical competencies through laboratory practice. New skills for leading and designing groups will be taught, and Module I and II skills will be refined and embedded in the group context.

The Launch:

At completion of training you will be ready to be launched and to begin "your" own group. You will be ready to begin the Planning Stage in your home CEC including the selection (or, possibly, completion) of a suitable design.

This final chapter is intended to summarize material presented in the book and to ready you for the next phase of learning (skill training in group employment counselling).

THE END: SUMMARY

The Model

At its best, a CEIC group is not only a small, cohesive community in which people feel received, accepted and challenged, but it is also a place with an atmosphere that allows people to become creative together in overcoming barriers to employment. Ideally, a CEIC group is a place for clients to acquire employment skills in a supportive learning structure.

In this text a model for group employment counselling was described which had five components:

- **Group Goals and Activities**
- **Member Needs and Roles**
- **Group Processes**
- **Leader Functions and Skills**
- **Design**

The nature of these components was described for each of the six Stages of Group Development:

- **Planning**
- **Initial**
- **Transition**
- **Working**
- **Termination**
- **Post-Group**

The ways that these components link together and the important characteristics of each component as the group evolves over time are summarized in Figure 5.

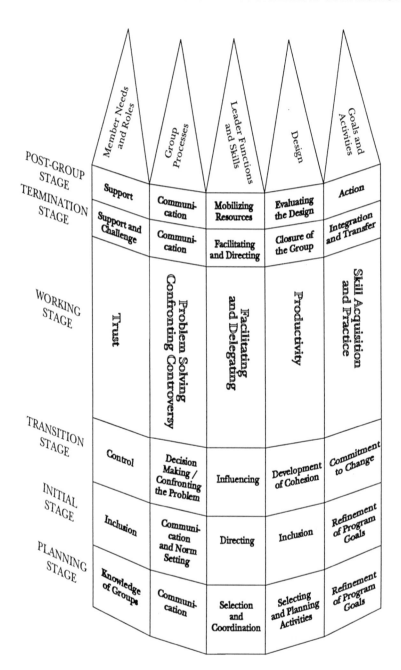

Figure 5. The Integrated Model

Leadership

There remain two aspects important to understanding the running of the group:

- First, remember that the group's development over time is not lock step and smooth. The group may be operating in more than one stage at a time, for instance: working on skill acquisition while still building inclusion. The group may actually regress slightly, at times, before it moves fully into the next developmental stage.

- Second, note that during each stage the leader's approach will change according to member needs, group goals and the group's maturity. A thorough understanding of the way groups develop over time is a necessary part of knowledge about groups and is essential for effective leadership.

These two points challenge you to adapt your approach and skills according to the evolving stages of group development.

An Effective Group

Knowledge of the group components and stages and the understanding of the use of leader skills in response to evolving member needs will result in the understanding of what constitutes an effective or ineffective group. The importance of these variables is brought into sharp focus as the differences between effective and ineffective groups are compared.

EFFECTIVE GROUPS	INEFFECTIVE GROUPS
Most members feel a sense of inclusion and excluded members are invited to become more active. Communication among most members is open and involves accurate expression of what is being experienced.	Many members feel excluded or cannot identify with other members. Cliques are formed and tend to lead to fragmentation. There is fear of expressing feelings or being left out.

(Effective Groups)	(Ineffective Groups)
Members accept the responsibility for deciding what action they will take to solve their problems.	Members blame others for their personal difficulties and aren't willing to take action to change.
Group members use out-of-group time to work on problems raised in the group.	Group members think about group activity very little when they are outside the group.
Communication is two way, and the open and accurate expression of both ideas and feelings is emphasized.	Communication is one-way and only ideas are expressed; feelings are ignored.
There is a willingness to risk disclosing threatening material; people become known. The interactions are honest and spontaneous. Members are willing to risk disclosing their reactions to others.	Participants hold back, and disclosure is at a minimum. Many members remain unknown.
Cohesion is high; there is a close emotional bond among people, common experiences. Members identify with one another. People are willing to risk experimental behaviour, because of the closeness and support.	Fragmentation exists; people feel distant from one another. There is a lack of caring or empathy. Members don't encourage one another to engage in new and risky behaviour, familiar ways are rigidly maintained.
Feedback is given freely and accepted without defensiveness. There is a willingness to reflect seriously on the accuracy of the feedback.	What little feedback is given is rejected defensively. Feedback is given without care or compassion.
Members feel hopeful; they feel that constructive change is possible.	Members feel despairing, helpless and trapped, victimized.

(Effective Groups)	(Ineffective Groups)
Goals are clarified and modified so that the best possible match between individual goals and the group's goals may be achieved; goals are cooperatively structured.	Members accept imposed goals; goals are competitively structured.
Group norms are developed cooperatively by the members and the leader. Norms are clear and designed to help the members attain their goals.	Norms are merely imposed by the leader and/or are not clear.
Participation and leadership among all group members; goal accomplishment, internal maintenance and developmental change are underscored.	Leadership is delegated and based upon authority; membership participation is unequal, with high-authority members dominating.
Controversy and conflict are seen as a positive key to members' involvement, the quality and originality of decisions, and the continuance of the group in good working condition.	Controversy and conflict are ignored, denied, avoided, or suppressed.
Conflict among members or with the leader is recognized, discussed, and most often, resolved.	Conflicts or negative feelings are ignored, denied, or avoided.
Decision-making procedures are matched with the situation: different methods are used at different times; consensus is sought for important decisions; involvement and group discussions are encouraged.	Decisions are always made by the highest authority; there is little group discussion; members' involvement is minimal.

(Effective Groups)	(Ineffective Groups)
Members evaluate the effectiveness of the group and decide how to improve its functioning. Goal accomplishment, internal maintenance, group processes, member roles, leader- ship design, and development are all considered important.	The highest authority evaluates the group's effectiveness and decides how goal accomplishment may be improved; internal maintenance and development are ignored as much as possible; stability is affirmed.

The above have been modified by the authors from separate lists, identified by Corey & Corey, 1982, (pp. 148-49) and Johnson & Johnson, 1982, (p. 11).

Preparation for the Launch: Training

What do you need to do to be "launched" into running an effective group? You need a period of preparation which is divided into two parts. Now that you have read this book and have understood the key concepts you have completed the first part.

The second part involves learning and practising group leadership skills in the next, training or workshop, phase of the module. On that occasion you will be challenged to try out leader skills by running simulation groups.

The Launch: Running Your Own Group

When all of this preparation is complete, your cognitive understanding will be integrated with skill acquisition. You will then be equipped to develop, implement and evaluate a group for the CEC Branch where you work. YOU WILL BE LAUNCHED!

EXERCISES

Using the material provided in Chapter VI, the Planning Stage, identify and characterize client needs which you think are particularly important in your community. Try to find a group which has not yet been widely identified.

Also, review Chapter V and bring design ideas, and any valuable exercises, to your training session. These ideas will be used to help you to select or design a group for your setting during the course of your training. Then you will be able to begin the Planning Stage when you arrive back at your own CEC setting.

Preparation for LAUNCH has begun...

References

Amundson, N.A. & Borgen. W.A. (1986). *A follow-up study of job search groups.* Unpublished manuscript.

Azrin, N.H., Philip, R.A., Thienes-Hontos, P. & Besalel, V.B. (1980). Comparative evaluation of the job club program with welfare recipients. *Journal of Vocational Behavior,* **16**, 133–145.

Borgen, W.A. & Amundson, N.A. (1984). *The experience of unemployment.* Toronto: Nelson Canada.

Borgen, W. A. & Amundson, N.A. (1987). The dynamics of unemployment. *Journal of Counselling and Development.* In press.

Canadian Guidance and Counselling Association. (1988). *An ethical standards casebook.* Toronto: Nelson.

Corey, G. & Corey, M.S. (1980). *Groups: Process and practice.* (2nd Edition). Monterey: Brooks/Cole.

Corey, G. (1985). *Theory and practice of group counselling.* (2nd Edition). Belmont, California: Wadsworth.

Dimock, G.D. (1976). *The series on leadership and group development.* Montreal: Concordia University.

Dinkmeyer, D.C. & Munro, J.J. (1971). *Group counseling: Theory and practice.* Itasco, IL: F.E. Peacock.

Egan, G. (1985). *The skilled helper* (2nd Edition). Monterey: Brooks Cole.

Fisher, B.A. (1974). *Small groups decision-making: Communication and the group process.* New York: McGraw-Hill.

Hare, A.P. (1976). *Handbook of small group research.* (2nd Edition). New York: The Free Press.

Hershey, P. & Blanchard, K. (1977). *Management of organizational behavior: Utilizing human resources.* (3rd Edition). Englewood Cliffs, NJ: Prentice-Hall.

Johnson, D. & Johnson, R. (1982). *Joining together: Group theory and group skills.* (2nd Edition). Englewood Cliffs, NJ: Prentice-Hall.

Keith, R.D., Engles, J.R. & Winborn, B.B. (1977). Employment-seeking preparation and activity. An experimental job placement training model for rehabilitation clients. *Rehabilitation Counselling Bulletin*, **21**, 159-165.

Kubler-Ross, E. (1969). *On death and dying*. New York: MacMillan.

Mahler, C.A. (1969). *Group counseling in the schools*. Boston: Houghton, Mifflin.

Maslow, A. (1968). *Toward a psychology of being*. (2nd Edition). Toronto: D. Van Nostrand Company (Canada) Ltd.

McWhirter, J., Nichols, E. & Banks, N. (1984). Career awareness and self-exploration (case) groups: A self-assessment model for career decision making. *The Personnel and Guidance Journal*, **62**, 580-582.

Ohlsen, M.M. (1970). *Group counselling*. New York: Holt, Rinehart and Winston.

Pfieffer, J.W. & Jones, J.E. (1977) (Eds.). *A handbook of structured experiences for human relations training*. (8 vols.). San Diego, CA: University Associates.

Schutz, W.C. (1958). *Firo: A three dimensional theory of interpersonal behavior*. New York: Holt, Rinehart & Winston.

Schutz, W.C. (1973). *Elements of encounter*. New York: Irvington.

Shulman, L. (1984). *Leading employment groups: A mutual aid approach*. Unpublished mimeo for the Employment Counselling Development Division, C.E.I.C.

Stanford, G. (1977). *Developing effective classroom groups*. New York: Hart.

Toffler. A. (1980). *The third wave*. New York: Bantam Books

Trotzer, J.P. (1977). *The counsellor and group: Integrating theory, training and practice*. Monterey: Brooks/Cole.

Tuckman. B. (1963). Developmental sequence in small groups. *Psychological Bulletin*, p. 384–399.